A SAINSBURY COOKBOOK

BRITISH COOKING
AT ITS BEST

GLYNN CHRISTIAN

D1513080

CONTENTS

Published exclusively for J Sainsbury plc
Stamford House Stamford Street
London SE1 9LL
by Woodhead-Faulkner Limited
Fitzwilliam House 32 Trumpington Street
Cambridge CB2 1QY

First published 1984
New enlarged edition 1985

Printed in Great Britain

THE AUTHOR

Glynn Christian is best known as the innovative and entertaining food reporter and chef on BBC TV's 'Breakfast Time'.

Born in New Zealand, where he worked as a radio and television writer, Glynn came to the United Kingdom in 1965. He developed his wide knowledge of ingredients and cooking while working as a travel writer throughout Europe. The success of his delicatessen on London's famed Portobello Road led to invitations to write extensively on delicatessen and speciality foods.

Glynn Christian broadcast original recipes for five years on London's LBC News Radio, and has also made three series for BBC TV's 'Pebble Mill at One', as well as being a regular broadcaster as one of 'Gloria's Gang', with Gloria Hunniford on BBC Radio 2. Glynn also writes regularly for *Over 21* and *Living* magazines.

A direct descendant of Fletcher Christian, who led the mutiny on HMS *Bounty*, Glynn also takes a strong interest in Pitcairn Island, home of the mutineers' descendants. His major books include *The Delicatessen Food Handbook, The Delicatessen Cookbook, The World Guide to Cheese* and *Fragile Paradise*, which is the first biography of Fletcher Christian.

INTRODUCTION

How difficult it is to describe what British cooking is really like. The adjectives commonly used are 'good' and 'plain', the latter being used as an insult as much as a compliment, sometimes with justice. Yet plain food cannot be bettered if its quality is right and the freshness palpable. And British food certainly wasn't all that plain for most of its history!

An interesting question to ponder is how the inherently conservative people of the British Isles have come to accept and encourage influences from all round the world throughout history, and still do so at an ever-increasing rate. You have only to consider that one entire generation, perhaps two, believe that Chinese take-away, tandoori chicken, spaghetti, kebabs and hamburgers are British. The generation just older than them will think longingly of British cooking as baked apples and sweet cured hams, of the mellowness of cinnamon and the bite of cloves in baking, and of peppery beef stews, without ever thinking that the ingredients which make them so special – the spices – are all imported from far-away eastern lands that they may never see.

The earliest cooking in Britain was meat roasted over flames, and gruels of grains, eventually extended and flavoured with vegetables and herbs. The first contact with spices was during the long Roman occupation, but once the Romans left and the Dark Ages cast their pall over Europe the British returned to a simpler style of food that adapted regularly as they were invaded from one quarter or another. The most monumental change came with the last successful invasion of these shores, by the Duke of Normandy, William the Conqueror. As well as introducing new and more luxurious styles of cooking, the Normans gave us new words for food. Though the men who husbanded the animals called them by their old names, pigs or sheep for instance, those allowed to eat them called them by their French names – *porc, mouton* and *boeuf*.

It was the Crusaders travelling in hope of salvation who reintroduced spices to Britain, and with them came also sugar, oranges, dried fruit, rose water and orange water. If you were to recreate the 1382 coronation banquet of Richard II and set it down in the streets of Islamic cities today, it would scarcely create a stir, for by the fourteenth century classic British food was heavy with spice, coloured with saffron and sandalwood, perfumed by the rose and orange flower, thickened with almonds and rich with wines. In a word, it was Arabic. Later the church – and wars – interfered, so that men were forbidden the use of spice on religious grounds.

The rise and fall of a dozen empires and kingdoms have made their contribution to British food; sometimes for fashion, sometimes for sense. The Hanoverian kings first popularised the heavy, boiled German puddings; and Prince Albert introduced the idea of a plum pudding at Christmas time, changing everyone's perception of this festival, just as the increasingly available turkey has lately done. The British Empire's possessions in India gave us curry, chutney and ketchup; colonies in the Southern Hemisphere sent tropical fruits, dried fruits and countless tons of butter, and so the British developed their renown for baking, biscuits and cakes.

In the twentieth century, increased travel has increased the scale of influences and their acceptance. Soon after the last war, Chinese and Indian restaurants began to flourish, and by the 1960s it seemed impossible to eat out without being in an Italian restaurant. In most small towns in the United Kingdom your choice is still the same – Chinese, Indian or Italian. When Cyprus had troubles in the 1970s, the kebab house movement began its assault on this country, quickly followed by the monster hamburger movement. Outrage at this is loud but unwarranted. For generations Britain has taken what has been offered, chewed it over and kept what it liked. The process is just faster right now!

I hope you will be surprised at this book. I was certainly surprised at how quickly foods which have been common for centuries can disappear. Why did we stop using rose water about 60 years ago, or stop flavouring our custards with bay leaf or orange? Who first thought you could make a genuine Irish stew or a Lancashire hotpot with lamb rather than with mutton? And it can't have been laziness that stopped people making raspberry vinegar, for it takes no effort at all. Is it a silly snobbishness that has led to the virtual disappearance of the once envied British puddings based on breadcrumbs? Perhaps it is just the rush of the twentieth century, and now that it is almost over it is time to reassess.

I hope you will use the recipes in this book judiciously, altering the proportion of ingredients as it suits you – but without moving away from the spirit of the dish. Spirit seems to me to be the great link between the extraordinarily different styles of British food over the centuries: there has always been a recognisable spirit of the age. Through this book we can follow our predecessors' footsteps with respect, with sense and with the lightness of our own touch.

Note on quantities

Ingredients in the recipes are given in both imperial (oz, fl oz, etc.) and metric (g, ml, etc.) measures. Use either set of quantities, but not a mixture of both, in any one recipe. All spoon measures are level spoons unless otherwise stated (metric spoon measures are always level). Egg size, where not specified, is medium (size 3).

FIRST COURSES

BARLEY BROTH

1½–2 oz (40–50 g) pearl barley

2½ pints (1.5 litres) stock or water mixed with 2 stock cubes

8 oz (225 g) mixed root vegetables, such as carrots, parsnips, turnips and celeriac, grated

1–2 whole cloves of garlic (optional)

Although it is generally associated with Scotland, there can be few households in Britain that have never made and enjoyed a barley broth. It's basically a good way to utilise the cooking liquid from boiled meat or vegetables; but it is delicious and sustaining enough to merit making from scratch, even if you use stock cubes. If you have time, soak the barley overnight, which will sweeten it. I toast the barley for extra colour and flavour.

Toast the pearl barley by stirring it over a medium heat in a non-stick pan. (Use a little oil if you do not have a non-stick surface.) Once the barley is an even brown, tip it out or it will burn.

A marvellous stock can be made for this broth by boiling up the bones of a roasted chicken together with root vegetables. Alternatively, if you soak the barley overnight the soaking water would make a good stock. The vegetables should include only a small amount of onion or celery, as both tastes tend to dominate. It is not traditional, but whole, unpeeled cloves of garlic are a delightful addition.

To make the broth, put the stock (or the water and stock cubes) with the grated vegetables, the garlic (if used) and the barley in a large saucepan. Cook gently for at least 1½ hours or until the barley is really tender and the broth is thickening.

WARM WATERCRESS, POTATO AND BACON SALAD

1 lb (450 g) small new potatoes

8 oz (225 g) streaky bacon

2 bunches of watercress, trimmed, washed and dried

2 tablespoons (2 × 15 ml spoon) sunflower oil

2 tablespoons (2 × 15 ml spoon) wine vinegar

Watercress is native to both Europe and Western Asia and has emigrated further afield with great success. Sometimes too great: in the waterways of my own native New Zealand it is a serious weed hazard. It needs a continual supply of cool running water to grow in, and commercially this means springs or boreholes for maximum purity. Hampshire is Britain's watercress capital: one firm there grows a quarter of the country's entire consumption. Use it as dark and as fresh as possible – it is then exceedingly rich in vitamin C.

Boil the potatoes in their skins. Slice the bacon, leaving its rind on, into 1–inch (2.5 cm) lengths. Fry to crisp in its own fat, in a non–stick pan. Divide the watercress into four helpings and put them on four large plates. Slice the warm or cold potatoes lengthways and put them on top of the watercress. Spoon out the bacon and sprinkle it on the potatoes. Add the sunflower oil and the wine vinegar to the bacon fat, bring to the boil, scrape up and sprinkle over the salads. Serve.

Warm Watercress, Potato and Bacon Salad
Potted Trout with Cucumber Scales

POTTED TROUT WITH CUCUMBER SCALES

1 large cucumber, sliced very thinly

1 dessertspoon (10 ml spoon) oil

½ teaspoon (2.5 ml spoon) ground mace

½ teaspoon (2.5 ml spoon) ground allspice

1 oz (25 g) onion, chopped finely

grated peel of 1 small lemon

1 oz (25 g) parsley, chopped

2 trout weighing about 1 lb (450 g), cleaned

½ bottle of white wine

4 oz (100 g) butter

salt, to taste

Trout is a comparatively new arrival on the everyday food scene, thanks to the growth in the number of fish farms. In medieval times every village and manor house had its own fish farm, but these disappeared during the Industrial Revolution and have only really reappeared as commercial ventures since the Second World War. You will see both pink and white fleshed trout for sale, so use either – there's no difference in the taste. Potting (which is the British word for pâté, if you like) is a good way of serving trout without the problem of bones, which some people find so tiresome. This delicately flavoured dish could be an important part of a light summer meal, or would make a superb start to a traditional British winter dinner.

Blanch the sliced cucumber in boiling water for 1 minute, drain, refresh in cold water and pat dry. Oil a bowl or bowls for the trout: it (or they) should be rounded, and hold 12–16 fl oz (350–480 ml) in total. Line the bowl(s) with overlapping cucumber slices, imitating fish scales as well as you can, and leaving some hanging over the edge at the top, ready to fold over the top of the filling.

In a large frying pan scatter the mace, allspice, chopped onion, lemon peel and chopped parsley; then lay the trout over the top. Pour on the white wine and bring up to a light simmer. Cover with foil and poach until the fish are just cooked, turning them over half-way through (they will need about 5 minutes on each side). Take out the fish. Remove their heads, skins and all their bones. Reserve the flesh and put the skin and bones (but not the head) back into the pan. Simmer for a further 5 minutes and then drain and sieve the cooking liquid. Let any heavy sediment settle out, pour the liquid back into the saucepan (through muslin or a fine strainer if you wish) and reduce over the heat to a few tablespoons.

Melt the butter. Mix together the melted

butter, the trout flesh and the reduced cooking liquid and mash well. Taste for seasoning. Press into the cucumber-lined bowl(s), fold over the cucumber edges and cover the remaining spaces with more cucumber slices. Chill for 3 hours, until set firmly, before unmoulding. Serve with lemon, horseradish and fresh brown bread and butter.

JERUSALEM ARTICHOKE AND SMOKED OYSTER SOUP

Serves 4–5

2 lb (900 g) jerusalem artichokes, peeled well and chopped

1 tablespoon (15 ml spoon) lemon juice

4 oz (105 g) can of smoked oysters in oil

1 oz (25 g) butter

2 large cloves of garlic, peeled

a little milk (optional)

5 fl oz (150 ml) carton of double cream

chopped parsley

salt and pepper

This knobbly vegetable, famous for being neither an artichoke nor for coming from Jerusalem, is in fact a member of the sunflower family. It is native to North America, where the French happened upon them in Massachusetts, and they had arrived in London via France by 1617. Jerusalem artichokes go marvellously with anything smoked, and smoked oysters have always been a great favourite of the British gentleman. This chowder-style soup will prove to be a favourite of all, I'm sure, gentlemen or not.

Place the chopped jerusalem artichokes in a saucepan and just cover with water. Add the lemon juice, the oil from the tin of oysters, the butter and the garlic cloves. Simmer gently until the artichoke pieces are tender.

Liquidise and then sieve all these ingredients, together with the cooking water. Taste the soup, adjust the seasoning and, if necessary, thin out with a little milk.

Whip the cream and chop the smoked oysters. Add the oysters to the cream, together with as much chopped parsley as you like. Serve the soup with 'islands' of this mixture spooned into the centre of each bowl.

PARSNIP AND APPLE SOUP

1 lb (450 g) parsnips, washed, trimmed (but unpeeled) and chopped roughly

8 oz (225 g) apples, cored and chopped (but unpeeled)

4 oz (100 g) onions, sliced thinly

2 oz (50 g) butter

1 pint (600 ml) water

2 chicken stock cubes

1–2 tablespoons (1–2 × 15 ml spoon) grated lemon rind

2 fresh bay leaves

1 pint (600 ml) milk

salt and pepper

Parsnips have been cultivated for at least 2,000 years. In medieval British cookery their prime use was as a source of sweetness: they were baked in sweet pies in honey or made into fritters. They were also widely used for feeding to pigs, as the resulting pork was then at its most aromatic and delicate: Parma ham, to this day, still comes from pigs fed on parsnips. In this delicious soup, the sweetness of parsnip is perfectly balanced by the sharp bite of apple. After I had 'invented' it, I discovered that it was in fact a traditional West Country soup, although there it is more likely to be flavoured with sage than lemon.

Soften the chopped parsnip, apple and onion in the butter for 10–15 minutes, using a covered pan over a low heat. Add the water to the pan with the 2 stock cubes, the lemon rind and the bay leaves; then leave to cook gently for 15–20 minutes or until all the ingredients are soft.

Remove the bay leaves, liquidise the soup and then sieve. Add the milk (or, if you prefer, substitute another pint of stock). Test for seasoning and add salt and pepper if necessary.

Jerusalem Artichoke and Smoked Oyster Soup
Parsnip and Apple Soup

SMOKED MACKEREL WITH HORSERADISH AND BEETROOT

Serves 2

2 large fillets or 2 small, whole, smoked mackerel

6 baby beetroots, boiled and peeled

horseradish sauce

There are two things wrong with smoked mackerel in this country. Firstly, very little of it is smoked authentically, and secondly, a great deal of it is made into a pasty pâté that is often overloaded with cream cheese. However you buy mackerel, filleted or not, one of the best ways to enjoy them is hot. As with so much British food, smoked mackerel served hot is ideal both as a main course for a light meal or as a starter for a larger one.

Use 1 large fillet or a small, whole smoked fish per person. Grill the mackerel for 10 minutes under a medium heat, turning it over half-way through if you are using whole fish. Serve them with the boiled beetroots and with horseradish sauce for a quick meal. They're delicious, too, with the Warm Watercress, Potato and Bacon Salad on page 8.

WICKED PASTA

Serves 4, or 6–8 as a starter

½ oz (15 g) packet of dried mushrooms

½ pint (300 ml) double cream

¼ pint (150 ml) white wine

1 lb (450 g) fresh green noodles or 8–12 oz (225–350 g) dried

6–8 oz (175–225 g) potted shrimps

salt

The greater availability of pasta, including fresh pasta, throughout the country means that a new generation is growing up seeing pasta as basic to the British diet. What a good idea!

This recipe is wicked because it is expensive, rich and unbelieveably easy to make – it seems a sin, somehow, to prepare something so good, so easily! The sauce is so rich you do not need much on the pasta, and this is the proper way to eat it.

English wine would be perfect in this recipe, and the potted shrimps add a delightful nutty flavour that nothing else could do (it must be nice for enthusiasts to find some other way to eat them than with toast). Incidentally, always send potted shrimps back if a restaurant serves them cold and congealed – they should be warm, dribbling with the spiced butter in which they were packed.

Put the dried mushrooms in a pan with the cream and simmer very gently for about 20 minutes until the mushrooms are softening. Then add the white wine and continue to simmer slowly until the mushrooms are really soft and the sauce has reduced by about a quarter. Keep warm.

Now cook the pasta in masses of boiling, salted water. Fresh pasta will be cooked in just a few minutes. If you can only get dried noodles, use 8–12 oz (225–350 g) depending on how hungry you are and follow the packet's directions.

Just as the pasta is ready, tip the shrimps into the mushroom sauce and warm through. Drain the noodles, serve, and ladle on the warm sauce.

ORANGE MUSHROOMS

Serves 2–3

1 lb (450 g) large mushrooms

2 cloves of garlic, chopped finely (optional)

4 oz (100 g) butter

4 tablespoons (4 × 15 ml spoon) orange juice

2 tablespoons (2 × 15 ml spoon) lemon juice

1 oz (25 g) parsley, chopped

Since mushrooms first began to be commercially cultivated on a large scale around 1947, they have become enormously popular, and rightly so. But don't forget that mushrooms aren't always button-sized: those are just immature mushrooms, and if they were to stay where they were they would eventually grow into big mushrooms, commercially known as 'opens' or 'flats'. These, for my money, have much more flavour than the little ones; and I think it's nice to enjoy them on their own, as a starter, rather than forever slicing them into a sauce at the last minute.

Remove the mushroom stems and either quarter the mushrooms or leave them whole, whichever you prefer. Chop the stems finely, with the garlic if you're using it (and it *is* good!). Melt the butter and gently fry the mushrooms for 3 minutes on each side. Add the stems (and garlic if used) and fry for a further 1½ minutes. Turn the heat up and add the orange and lemon juice; then let the sauce bubble thoroughly. Add the parsley and mix through. Serve each mushroom or the mushroom quarters with the sauce poured over the top. The bread you use to soak up the juices will not need butter!

SEAFOOD IN PASTRY WITH LEEK CREAM SAUCE

12 oz–1 lb (350–450 g) puff pastry

1 egg yolk

1 sachet of powdered saffron

12 oz (350 g) trimmed leeks, sliced thinly, using a lot of the green part

½ pint (300 ml) single or double cream

6 oz (175 g) mussels, fresh or canned in brine

6 oz (175 g) cockles, fresh or canned in brine

about 2 oz (50 g) butter

a little wine or vermouth (optional)

1 clove of garlic, chopped finely (optional)

salt and pepper

To garnish:

chopped parsley (optional)

Oven temperature:
Gas Mark 7/425°F/220°C

Seafood in Pastry with Leek Cream Sauce ▶

Lightly flavoured food served in featherlight puff pastry has become firmly established as a new style of first course. I think no combination is better than pastry and seafood, so here I recommend using our delicious mussels and cockles, but prawns or even scampi would be just as good. The sauce is simple to make and is a stunning sea-green. Serve everything warm rather than hot, for maximum flavour.

Preheat the oven. Roll out the pastry into a rectangle and cut out 6 rectangles, about 5 × 3 inches (13 × 8 cm) – this will be a little thicker than you usually roll pastry. Mix the egg yolk with the saffron and paint each pastry shape. Using a sharp–pointed knife, make an even criss-cross pattern on the top of each. Bake on a lightly wetted tray in the preheated oven for 10–15 minutes until very well risen and cooked through. Cool a little, split carefully in two, remove any uncooked pastry and return to the turned-off, cooling oven to dry out.

Cook the sliced leek over a gentle heat in the cream until well softened but still rather green. Liquidise and then strain through a fine sieve. Season and keep warm.

If you are using mussels or cockles, neither should have been bathed in vinegar and both should be rinsed well to remove any remaining grains of sand. Melt enough butter in a pan to coat the seafood, with a little wine or vermouth, if used. Toss the seafood in this just long enough to warm through. (Those with a taste for the earth rather than the sea might also sprinkle in a little finely chopped garlic!)

Put the bottom of each reheated pastry sandwich in the middle of a warm plate and pile on the seafood. Sandwich with the pastry tops. Now spoon the warm leek cream around the pastry. Sprinkle a little chopped parsley on the sauce and serve at once.

POTTED HARE

1 lb (450 g) skinned hare pieces (legs are suitable)

½ bottle of red wine

1 shallot, chopped finely

1 heaped teaspoon (1–2 × 5 ml spoon) thyme

1 clove of garlic, chopped finely

2 fresh bay leaves

6 juniper berries

3 allspice berries, crushed

3 oz (75 g) piece of smoked fatty bacon, chopped into cubes

4 oz (100 g) butter, melted

salt (optional)

Most people would recognise this as a pâté, but I have given it its correct, British name. You will find that the method used to make it is very different from, and much simpler than, the complicated water-bath baking and pressing used for pâté. It makes a wonderful starter, as this way, since hare is both uncommon and pricey, everyone gets a taste while the expense is kept to a minimum.

Marinate the hare pieces in the red wine, shallot, thyme, garlic, bay leaves, juniper and allspice berries for 24 hours.

Cook the bacon cubes slowly in a thick frying pan until all the fat is rendered – this will take a good half-hour. When this has happened, transfer the bacon to a saucepan. Remove the hare from the marinade and dry the pieces thoroughly. Brown them well in the bacon fat over a medium to high heat. Put the hare in a saucepan, pour away the browning fat and deglaze the frying pan by adding the marinade and stirring to dissolve all the solids left in the pan, scraping the bottom of the pan as you do so. Add all to the saucepan, bring up to simmering point and then cover the pan. Simmer gently until the hare is cooked: this will take 40–50 minutes, depending on the size of the pieces.

When the hare is cooked, remove it and allow to cool slightly. While the hare is cooling, reduce the cooking juices to about 6 tablespoons (6 × 15 ml spoon). Take all the hare meat carefully off the bone. Remove the bay leaves from the reduced cooking liquid and, if you wish, the juniper berries. Chop, mince or process the hare meat with the cooking liquid to the consistency you wish – perhaps chop or process two thirds very finely and one third more coarsely. Add salt, if necessary. Mix with 2 oz (50 g) of the melted butter and pot, either as one or in individual ramekins. Cover with the other 2 oz (50 g) of melted butter.

MAIN COURSES

ORANGE-BRAISED PIGEONS IN NESTS OF SPRING GREENS

Serves 2

2 prepared fresh or frozen wood pigeons

2 oz (50 g) butter

2 oz (50 g) onion, chopped finely

1–2 large cloves of garlic, chopped

1 dessertspoon (10 ml spoon) grated orange rind

6 dessertspoons (6 × 10 ml spoon) fresh orange juice

2 dessertspoons (2 × 10 ml spoon) fresh lemon juice

1 fresh bay leaf

8 oz (225 g) trimmed spring greens

salt

There can't be many food items that we all buy from time to time having only the vaguest idea of what it is we are buying, but 'spring greens' are probably one of them. They are essentially heartless cabbages, either from genuinely unhearting varieties or from hearting varieties taken young. They can even be young shoots taken from old cabbage plants, cauliflower or sprouts. The younger and greener, the better. Their delicious flavour is perfect with the fleshy breasts of our pigeons, much underrated of late, but now enjoying a fashionable return.

Press firmly down on the breasts of the pigeons to snap the rib cages and flatten them slightly. Cut out the backbones with kitchen scissors, leaving the rest of the ribs and the legs on, and open the pigeons as flat as possible. Trim off loose pieces of skin and pat dry all over.

Melt the butter over a medium heat and cook the chopped onion and garlic until soft, but avoid browning. Add the orange rind and citrus juices and continue cooking uncovered until most of the juices have evaporated. Push the onion to one side and then lightly brown the pigeon breasts. Redistribute the onion, turn the pigeon breasts uppermost and add the bay leaf; then cover and braise over a medium to low heat for 35–45 minutes, basting with the orange butter from time to time.

About 15 minutes before serving, wash and slice the greens thinly and cook in a little boiling salted water until wilted and soft but still a bright green. Arrange in a circle on two hot plates. Place a pigeon in the middle of each and then strain the cooking liquid (discarding the onions) over the greens.

BOILED BACON WITH GARLIC-ORANGE SAUCE

Serves 4–6

3 lb (1.3 kg) rolled bacon
joint

a 1¾-pint (1-litre) carton of
orange juice

2 teaspoons (2 × 5 ml
spoon) pickling spice

extra whole cloves, if
necessary

1 cinnamon stick

at least 2 unpeeled garlic
cloves per person

2 bay leaves

rind of 1 orange cut in
julienne strips

1 oz (25 g) coarsely chopped
parsley

*Boiled bacon is one of my favourite things – mainly
because you also end up with a wonderful stock in
which to cook other things or with which to make a
soup. The spiced orange stock used here has the
additional attraction of being a delightful colour,
making this a recipe suited both to sunny summer days
and dreary winter ones. You can use smoked or
unsmoked bacon, but smoked joints will give a more
unusual and interesting result. The long cooking also
reduces the effect of the garlic and each clove of it ends
up sweet and unctuous, almost like a mayonnaise.*

Put the bacon joint in a pan of cold water, bring
to the boil, simmer for a few minutes and then
remove the joint and throw away the water.
Return the bacon to the pan, add all the orange
juice and enough water to cover the joint by
about 1 inch. Put in the spices, garlic and bay
leaves. If the pickling spice mixture you add
includes less than 6 whole cloves, make up to
that number. Cover the pan, and once it is
simmering, cook the joint for 25 minutes per
pound plus 25 minutes.

About 20 minutes before the time is up, strain
off ½ pint (300 ml) of the cooking liquid,
remove all the garlic cloves, and reserve them.
Add the orange rind to the strained liquid and
poach gently. Then add the garlic cloves and
keep warm while you slice the bacon. Reheat the
sauce, and just before serving add the parsley. Be
sure the sauce is served over the meat slices,
so the parsley and garlic cloves remain on
them and the orange sauce spreads
on to the plate to frame each
portion.

Stuffed Cabbage in a Pastry Case

Orange-braised Pigeons in Nests of Spring Greens

Boiled Bacon with Garlic-orange Sauce

21

STUFFED CABBAGE IN A PASTRY CASE

Serves 6

1½ lb (675 g) green cabbage (trimmed weight)

4 tablespoons (4 × 15 ml spoon) olive oil

2 oz (50 g) finely chopped onion

2 oz (50 g) currants

3 oz (75 g) dried apricots, sliced

6 oz (175 g) long grain rice

2 heaped tablespoons (3 × 15 ml spoon) ground almonds

2 heaped tablespoons (3 × 15 ml spoon) chopped fresh mint

12 oz (350 g) packet of frozen puff pastry

1 egg

1 sachet of saffron powder

salt and pepper, to taste

To garnish:

1 lb (450 g) carton of natural yogurt

2–4 oz (50–100 g) melted butter

hot paprika or harissa sauce, to taste

Oven temperature:
Gas Mark 6/400°F/200°C

Nowadays the vegetarian is no longer considered an eccentric, and many people include vegetarian dishes in their normal diets. But vegetarians can feel rather left out at important traditional times, like Christmas, when the rest of the world celebrates with large joints or roasted birds. So I created this combination which may be brought to the table and sliced there, but which doesn't pretend to be meat. This recipe uses ingredients which are traditionally associated with the British Christmas and British cooking, but the dish that results is thoroughly in tune with modern styles of eating.

Cut out the central core of the cabbage and carefully detach the leaves. Blanch them 4 or 5 at a time in boiling water for two minutes then plunge into cold water. Keep 8 fl oz (240 ml) of the cabbage water.

Heat the oil in a large, heavy pan, and cook the onion until it is soft and starting to colour. Add the currants, apricots and rice, stir well, then pour in the reserved cabbage water. Cover the pan and cook without stirring until the water level has disappeared beneath the surface of the rice. Turn off the heat, cover tightly with a folded tea towel and the lid, then leave to steam for 15 minutes undisturbed. Meanwhile, cut the tough rib out of each cabbage leaf, going no further than half-way up each leaf. Dry each leaf thoroughly. Fluff up the rice, mix in the almonds and the mint, (use half as much dried mint if you have no fresh) and season to taste. Roll the pastry out to an oblong of about 18 inches × 12 inches (50 cm × 30 cm). Mix the egg with the saffron.

Stuff the cabbage leaves by putting a tablespoon (15 ml spoon) of the mixture into the centre of each. Fold in the sides of the leaf and then roll the parcels up tightly. Sit the parcels on their seams so they do not unroll.

Pile the stuffed cabbage rolls upside-down

(with the seams uppermost) in a smaller oblong in the centre of the pastry. The pile should be about three layers high and must not make a pyramid shape: the top layer must be as flat and as wide as the bottom one. This is simply done by swapping different shapes around to get a balance.

Fold the pastry over, folding and tucking the edges back over the top like a parcel, as in the diagram. Trim off any obvious excess, then seal the joins very well with a little moisture and pressure. The finished 'package' should be about 8 × 5 × 5 inches (20 × 12.5 × 12.5 cm). Turn the parcel over and onto a baking tray then use the tip of a sharp-pointed knife to etch a pattern into the pastry. Parallel lines or diamonds made by intersecting diagonals look best. Cut two small air vents right through the pastry, then paint the lot with the saffron–egg glaze.

Bake for 35–45 minutes, to ensure the pastry base is cooked through.

Slice the roll with a very sharp knife. Top with generous blobs of chilled natural yogurt, then bathe each with hot, melted butter which you have mixed with either hot paprika or a dab or two of harissa sauce, or some other hot sauce.

A GOOSE WITH GOLDEN APPLES

1 oven-ready goose, weighing about 9–10 lb (4–4.5 kg)

1–2 onions, chopped

2 cloves of garlic, crushed

1 large lemon, sliced

1–1½ pints (600–900 ml) dry cider

1 teaspoon (5 ml spoon) ground cinnamon

1–2 pinches of ground cloves

½ teaspoon (2.5 ml spoon) ground nutmeg

1–2 oz (25–50 g) butter

For the apples:

8 small golden delicious apples

4 oz (100 g) ground almonds

1 teaspoon (5 ml spoon) sugar, plus a little extra

1 sachet of powdered saffron, plus a little extra

½–1 teaspoon (1–2 × 2.5 ml spoon) orange flower water

1 dessertspoon (10 ml spoon) currants

1 egg yolk

Oven temperature:
Gas Mark 4/350°F/180°C

This is truly the British festive bird, favoured for generations before the upstart turkey from North America arrived in the seventeenth century. You need a big goose, for, like ducks, geese are deceptively low on flesh: allow at least 1 lb (450 g) of uncooked bird per person.

Teaming a goose with apples is always successful. Here I have used a stuffing with a medieval flavour and gilded the apples just the way they did in those times. It looks and tastes stunning.

Remove the excess fat from inside the bird. Put the chopped onion, crushed garlic and sliced lemon inside the bird. Boil the cider with the spices, pour over the bird and marinate for at least 4 hours, or overnight if that is simpler. Spoon over the marinade regularly, and ensure that there is plenty inside the bird. If you have refrigerated it or taken it from a cold larder, let it stand to reach room temperature before cooking. Pour off the marinade and keep it to one side, but leave the vegetables inside the bird. Preheat the oven.

Roast the goose on a rack in a pan for 15 minutes per pound (450 g). It has a better and sweeter taste when still a little pink. During cooking, pour off the fat and reserve it, but do not baste the bird.

Brown the giblets in a little of the goose fat, add all of the marinade and cook over a medium heat for about 45 minutes, or until it is rich and starting to reduce. Strain through muslin or a very fine sieve, and keep warm.

Core the apples and score a line right round them through the skin, about one third from the top. Mix the almonds, sugar, saffron, orange flower water and currants together with a spoonful or more of the hot goose fat and stuff

A Goose with Golden Apples

the apples. Dribble more goose fat over them, and bake in an ovenproof dish at the bottom of the oven for 30–45 minutes – they should be only just done when the goose is ready.

Once the goose is ready, take it from the pan and leave to stand, covered lightly, for at least 15 minutes, so that it sets nicely. Pour off the remaining fat from the pan and add any accumulated cooking juices to the giblet-marinade gravy, and reduce this further so that there are a few spoons of sauce per person.

A few minutes before you are ready to serve, carefully remove the top part of the cooked skin of the apples, revealing the white cooked pulp. Mix the egg yolk with the extra saffron and the extra touch of sugar. Paint this mixture over the exposed apples and replace in the oven for just 5 or so minutes until set. Whisk the 1–2 oz (25–50 g) butter into the sauce over a medium heat.

Arrange the goose with its golden apples on a serving dish, pour the spiced sauce into a hot jug and take to your festive table.

BLACK PUDDING WITH SPINACH, APPLE AND CURRANTS

2 dessertspoons (2 × 10 ml spoon) butter

1 oz (25 g) chopped shallot or onion

2 small or 1 large Cox's Orange Pippin, peeled, cored and sliced thinly

1 tablespoon (15 ml spoon) currants

1½ lb (750 g) fresh spinach

about 1 lb (450 g) black pudding

freshly ground nutmeg

Perhaps one of the world's oldest treats, black pudding, or blood sausage, is especially associated with the North of England. It is also immensely popular, however, in Scotland and Ireland, where it is known as drisheen. Rich with barley or oats and chunks of pork fat in Lancashire and Yorkshire, British puddings change once they are made closer to the Border or north of it, for up there they prefer a smoother pudding without the chewy pieces of pork.

Black pudding is already well-cooked, so it may be eaten cold and is excellent spread like a pâté on biscuits or bread. But here I've combined hot pudding with some of the ingredients other countries serve with their puddings or, even, put into them. It makes a substantial lunch or supper dish that is a stunning contrast of bright colours and friendly flavours.

Melt the butter and cook the shallot or onion in it until soft and golden. Add the apples and the currants, cover, and cook gently until the apple has softened but is still keeping its shape. Do not let the mixture brown too much. Once ready, keep warm.

Wash the spinach thoroughly, shake it dry and put it into a large saucepan. Cook over a medium heat, turning from time to time until it is evenly tender and a rich, bright green. Drain away any excess liquid, then combine the spinach with the apple mixture. Prick the black pudding and put it into hot (not boiling) water, bring it to the boil, and simmer a few minutes to heat through.

Put the spinach mixture onto a plate or plates and grate over some nutmeg. Slice the pudding thickly on the diagonal, arrange on the spinach and serve at once.

MINTED SADDLE OF LAMB WITH LAVERBREAD SAUCE

Serves 6–8

1 large bunch of fresh mint

6–7 lb (2.5–3 kg) saddle of lamb

garlic, sliced (optional)

½ pint (300 ml) dry white vermouth

a few knobs of butter

For the sauce:

8 oz (225 g) can of laverbread

grated rind and juice of 1 orange

garlic, to taste

grated nutmeg, to taste

salt and pepper

To garnish:

mint leaves
orange slices, (optional)

Oven temperature:
Gas Mark 4/350°F/180°C

Our 'traditional' mint sauce made with vinegar or lemon juice more properly belongs to mutton; it was always a jelly or sauce made with the sharp red berries of rowan or currants that used to accompany lamb. But as fashion changed, and mutton became less widely available, mint sauce remained.

The technique used here of roasting lamb on a bed of mint and then making a sauce of the cooking juices, aided by alcohol, is one which can be adapted to a shoulder or leg of lamb. The addition of an orange and laverbread sauce gives a Welsh flavour to this dish, and it can be used with other lamb dishes. Use either the laverbread sauce or the minty sauce, or both together, as here.

Next time you have a crowd to please, serve a saddle. It looks important, and has the advantage of being easier to carve than either shoulder or leg. The saddle here should stand for at least 5 hours before cooking, so allow plenty of time.

Put about two thirds of the mint, stalk and all, under the flaps of the saddle and fold the flaps under to enclose the mint. Make a series of small pockets between the skin and the flesh, rather than deep into the meat. Stuff these with mint, too, but in this case use just the leaves rather than the stalks. Reserve a few nice mint leaves for garnishing. Slivers of garlic can be incorporated into these pockets. Leave the prepared saddle in a cool place, but not the refrigerator, for at least 5 hours so that the flavours can permeate. (On a weekend you could do this the night before.)

Preheat the oven. Put the saddle on a small rack that will fit in your roasting dish and put directly into the preheated oven. The rack is vital – if you do not use one, the underneath of the meat will stew rather than roast. If you like meat which is cooked through, cook for 20 minutes per pound (450 g); for meat which is pink, 15 minutes per pound (450 g) is adequate, as long as

Minted Saddle of Lamb with Laverbread Sauce ▶

the joint was at room temperature when you began to cook it and as long as you do not leave the oven door open while basting.

Half-way through the cooking time, heat the vermouth to boiling point and pour it over the saddle. From then on, you should baste well every half-hour.

The prepared laverbread is now simply mixed with the grated rind and juice of the orange, and further flavoured with generous quantities of garlic, grated nutmeg, salt and pepper, to your individual taste. Simmer gently to soften the rawness of the peel and garlic; then set aside.

Once the meat is cooked, take it off the rack, recover any mint from under the flaps and save it; then cover the joint lightly and let it stand for 15–20 minutes. Pour off the fat from the pan, place over a medium heat, add the mint from the meat and scrape the bottom. As soon as you have a rich brown colour, boil for a little longer and then strain, pressing out all the juices from the mint. Before serving, whisk in some knobs of butter to shine and thicken the sauce somewhat. Reheat the laverbread sauce and pour around the meat. Garnish with mint leaves and orange slices, if you like. Carve along the length of the saddle in long slices as shown in the diagram, and serve with the minty sauce.

PECULIARLY GOOD OXTAIL

Serves 6, though it's so good I've seen 2 finish it!

8 tablespoons (8 × 15 ml spoon) olive oil

2 oxtails, chopped into 2-inch (5 cm) lengths and trimmed of all excess fat

seasoned flour

4 celery stalks, cut into 1-inch (2.5 cm) lengths

1 bottle of Theakston's 'Old Peculier' or other strong beer

Although classic oxtail soups and stews are delicious, they are not terribly popular nowadays. There seem to be two reasons for this: the first is that they are rich fare and make rather heavy eating, and the second, connected, reason is that they are high in fat, which worries more and more cooks nowadays. I've created the following recipe with these problems in mind. Its outstanding features are the use of celery, a magically successful partner for oxtail, and the use of beer and tomatoes, which, with their natural acids, give a more balanced taste and a prettier look to the final dish. I've also cut down and balanced the fats and oils that go into

1¾ lb (775 g) or 2 × 14 oz
(397 g) can of tomatoes

2 bay leaves

6 cloves of garlic, unpeeled

the dish, so that you can now unlock the past without
imperilling your future!

Heat half the olive oil in a heavy frying pan. Toss
the oxtail pieces in seasoned flour, and then fry
them until a golden colour. Remove and discard
any remaining oil or flour.

Heat the rest of the oil in the same pan, add the
celery sticks and cook until they begin to soften
slightly. Pour on the Old Peculier and allow to
bubble through, scraping the pan as you do so.

In a large casserole layer the pieces of oxtail,
the celery and ale, the tomatoes, the bay leaves
and the garlic. The liquid should just cover all
the meat. Bring to a gentle simmer on top of the
stove and cook slowly for 1½–2 hours, until the
meat comes away very easily from the bones.

COTTAGE PIE AND SHEPHERD'S PIE

Serves 4–6

1 small onion, chopped
finely

1 lb (450 g) minced beef,
chopped lamb, or meat
leftovers

1 tablespoon (15 ml spoon)
oil

¾ oz (20 g) plain flour

¼ pint (150 ml) brown
stock

1 tablespoon (15 ml spoon)
chopped parsley

a pinch of marjoram or
lovage

1 teaspoon (5 ml spoon)
Worcestershire sauce

1 lb (450 g) cooked, mashed
and buttered potatoes

salt and pepper

Oven temperature:
Gas Mark 4/350°F/180°C

*These two dishes are often thought to be the same
thing: leftover roast meat baked in some sort of sauce or
gravy under a topping of mashed potatoes. In fact,
ideally, both should be made with fresh meat – and the
Shepherd's Pie, not surprisingly, should be made with
lamb (it would have been mutton in the old days).
Another distinction sometimes made between the two
is that the beef of the Cottage Pie should be minced,
whereas the lamb of the Shepherd's Pie should be
chopped or even sliced. An interesting variation of
both is Vicarage Pie, where the topping is of mashed
and buttered parsnips rather than potatoes.*

Preheat the oven. Brown the onion and the meat
– if you are using fresh meat – in the oil.
Leftovers should not be browned. Stir in the
flour and cook for a minute or two more. Add
the stock and simmer through for a minute or
two. Add the rest of the ingredients, including
the leftover meat if used. Season. Put this
mixture in a baking dish and cover with the
potatoes, marking their surface with a fork.
Bake in the preheated oven for 45 minutes until
the potatoes are nicely browned on top.

BACON HOCK WITH PEASE PUDDING

2½–3 lb (1.25–1.3 kg) bacon hock

2 onions, sliced

1 lb (450 g) pease pudding, prepared

3 eggs

1–2 oz (25–50 g) butter, softened

3 tablespoons (3 × 15 ml spoon) chopped parsley

One of the reasons, perhaps, why pease pudding isn't so popular now is because of the forward planning required: the hours of soaking followed by the hours of cooking. But don't forget that pulses are just as good canned as fresh, and pease pudding is no exception to this rule. You can eat it, heated, just as it comes out of the can if you wish, but the traditional way is to put eggs and fat or butter into it, and then to bake or boil it – and that's just what I've done here. Try serving with sliced root vegetables.

Put the bacon hock in a large saucepan with the sliced onion and cover with cold water. (As bacon hock is not very salty, you will not need to discard the water.)

Put the pease pudding in a mixing bowl and beat the eggs and softened butter into it. Line a small bowl with 3 or 4 long strips of cling film at right angles to each other. Add the pease pudding mixture and fold the ends of the cling film over the top. Invert this package on to another 2 or 3 sheets of cling film and seal again. Then put the parcel on a sheet of foil, pull up and seal the edges. Repeat once more with another sheet of foil. Add this package to the saucepan as soon as the water cooking the meat comes to the boil. Cook together until the meat is done (the pease pudding package will float). Cook for 25 minutes per pound (450 g), plus 25 minutes.

When the meat is ready, take out the pease pudding. Carefully remove the foil (which may contain some water) and the cling film. Remove the rind from the hock, and slice both it and the pease pudding. Pour a few ladles of the cooking liquid on to the chopped parsley in a bowl. Place alternate slices of hock and pease pudding on serving plates, and serve with just enough parsley sauce to moisten.

Bacon Hock with Pease Pudding

WHITING WITH COCKLE AND HORSERADISH SAUCE

½ pint (300 ml) milk

2 oz (50 g) onion, sliced

1 bay leaf

6 black peppercorns

4 whiting, weighing about 12 oz (350 g) each

1 oz (25 g) parsley stalks

1 pint (600 ml) water

8 oz (225 g) cockles, plain or brined

2 dessertspoons (2 × 10 ml spoon) lemon juice (optional)

2½ oz (65 g) butter

1½ oz (40 g) flour

5 teaspoons (5 × 5 ml spoon) horseradish cream

1 lb (450 g) leeks, sliced very finely

salt and pepper, to taste

To garnish:

a small parsley leaf

Oven temperature:
Gas Mark 3/325°F/170°C

The whiting is one of the most underrated fish on our stalls – and I'm not sure why. Its flesh runs the far more expensive sole a respectable second, in terms of both texture and sweetness. It is also a very versatile fish to cook with: as well as being good served by itself – grilled, poached or deep-fried – it is also excellent for using in fish forcemeats, stuffings and quenelles. Whiting often used to be served biting their own tails (perhaps because they are rather long and thus could be better accommodated on a plate) and you'll sometimes see them displayed like this at the fishmonger's.

Gently heat the milk with 1 oz (25 g) of the sliced onion, the bay leaf and the black peppercorns until it just comes to the boil. Let it stand and steep for 15 minutes. Keep to one side.

Fillet the whiting by cutting off their heads and tails, chopping off their fins and gills and slicing down each side of the backbone to produce 2 fillets. These may be skinned if you wish. Make a fish stock, either by pressure cooking the fish trimmings with the remaining sliced onion, parsley stalks and the water at high pressure for 3 minutes, or by simmering the same ingredients in a large saucepan over a gentle heat for 25 minutes.

Meanwhile, wash the cockles to get rid of the grit and brine: put them first in a sieve and then put the sieve in a deep bowl. Fill with cold water, agitate the cockles well to release the grit and then lift the sieve full of cockles out of the water – leaving the grit in the bottom of the bowl. Do this four or five times; then give them a final rinse. Toss in the lemon juice, unless your cockles were preserved in vinegar, in which case they won't need it. Preheat the oven.

Make a roux by combining 1½ oz (40 g) of the butter and the flour over a medium heat. Stir for 5 minutes without letting it brown. When the roux is fully cooked, remove from the heat. Strain the milk (discarding the stalks, etc.) and whisk it into the roux gradually (no more than 4 tablespoons (4 × 15 ml spoon) at a time) followed by ½ pint (300 ml) of the fish stock. Return to the heat and cook the sauce through, reducing it to a thick texture.

Grease a large baking tray with the remaining butter. Place the whiting fillets in the tray and smear each fillet with about ½ teaspoon (2.5 ml spoon) of the creamed horseradish. Cover with the other ½ pint (300 ml) stock, place foil over the tray and bake in the preheated oven for about 20 minutes, or until the fillets are cooked but still firm.

Meanwhile, put the sliced leeks in a saucepan on their own, with no water and no fat. Cook them, stirring, over a medium heat until the liquid they will express has all steamed off: they will be bright green and squeaky-clean. Remove the saucepan from the heat immediately.

Take as much cooking stock from the cooked fillets as you need to give the fish stock sauce a nice coating texture; then season and add the final teaspoon (5 ml spoon) horseradish and the cockles to the sauce. Heat the sauce through fully. Place the fillets on a bed of the green leek and pour over the sauce. Garnish with the little parsley leaf.

LANCASHIRE HOT-POT

2 bay leaves

2 lb (900 g) potatoes, sliced finely

8 oz (225 g) onions, chopped finely

5 tablespoons (5 × 15 ml spoon) oil

1 oz (25 g) plain flour

2 lb (900 g) best-end lamb chops

1 pint (600 ml) water, or ½ pint (300 ml) water mixed with ½ pint (300 ml) strong dark beer

2 dessertspoons (2 × 10 ml spoon) Worcestershire sauce

1 teaspoon (5 ml spoon) anchovy sauce

6 lamb's kidneys

salt and pepper

Oven temperatures:
Gas Mark 7/425°F/220°C
Gas Mark 3/325°F/170°C

As is the case with Irish stew, just combining lamb chops, potato and some liquid will never give you an authentic Hot-pot. Hot-pots need the flavour of mutton and always used to include kidneys; indeed, they always used to have oysters in as well, though this – in those days – was a gesture to economy, as oysters were splendidly plentiful and cheap. Hot-pots were also quite highly flavoured with Worcestershire and Lancashire sauces. Again, as with Irish stew, if you are going to be using lamb rather than mutton – and it's generally Hobson's choice in this respect nowadays – then you are already adapting and moving away from the original flavour. Even so, this version should be closer to the Hot-pots of yesterday than most you will have tasted.

Preheat the oven to the higher setting. Put the bay leaves at the bottom of a large soufflé or casserole dish and place on top of them 1¼ lb (550 g) of the finely sliced potatoes. Season. Brown the finely chopped onion in 2 tablespoons (2 × 15 ml spoon) oil. Take out the onion, and reserve. Lightly flour the chops and brown them in the rest of the oil. Pour off any excess oil. Then add the water (or mixed water and beer) to the frying pan, scraping up the burnt meat and onion juices. Add the Worcestershire sauce and anchovy sauce to this stock, and season to taste.

Slice the kidneys in half across their middles. Layer the chops on the bottom layer of potatoes in the dish, packing them fairly tightly together. Put a kidney half on top of each chop and a small heap of cooked onion on top of each kidney half. Season. Add the final layer of potatoes, season and then pour on the stock. Cover the Hot-pot with foil and bake in the preheated oven for half an hour; then at the lower setting for 1½ hours. Take the foil off the top to allow the potatoes to brown for the last three quarters of an hour.

Lancashire Hot-pot

MUSTARD-OATMEAL COD STEAKS

Serves 2

2 dessertspoons (2 × 10 ml
spoon) coarse oatflakes

1 dessertspoon (10 ml
spoon) wholegrain mustard

1 teaspoon (5 ml spoon)
softened butter

2 cod steaks weighing about
6 oz (175 g) each

a little salt and pepper

Oven temperature:
Gas Mark 4/350°F/180°C

*Fish is enjoying a great resurgence of popularity – and
so it should! It is virtually fatless and thus offers
first-class protein with few calories. It's also very
versatile and cooks so quickly you save on energy
costs.*

*This recipe makes a really nourishing slimmer's
meal, but you can make it even more wickedly
delicious by doubling the butter in the topping and
serving the cod steaks on a bed of cooked spinach,
buttered if you like.*

Preheat the oven. Mix together the oats,
mustard and butter, and add a little salt and
pepper if you like. Lightly season the fish, then
smear the oatmeal mixture evenly onto the top
sides only of the two steaks.

Bake for 15–20 minutes depending on how
thick the steaks are; a squeeze or two of fresh
orange juice is a tangy way to add even more
appeal.

WELSH SALT DUCK

Serves 4

1 prepared 4–5 lb (1.8–
2.2 kg) duck

4 oz (100 g) fine (not
coarse) rock salt

2 oz (50 g) light muscovado
sugar

½ oz (15 g) saltpetre

2 bay leaves

onion

lemon

*This is quite an extraordinary dish, since its closest
relative is Chinese: Chinese Salted Duck is made
virtually the same way. It is delicious, particularly
when cold. Traditionally it was served with a rather
heavy onion sauce, made by combining a purée of
cooked onions with a thick white sauce. Do this if you
like, but I have found it more to the modern taste to
serve it with a purée of turnips and with fresh green
peas, both being traditional accompaniments to non-
salted duck. Allow 2 days for standing the duck
beforehand.*

Remove all excess fat from the duck and cut off
its tail, leaving it whole. Mix the salt, sugar and
saltpetre together and rub the duck all over with
this mixture, both inside the cavity and all over

the skin. Leave in a cool place for 2 days or more, re-rubbing the duck with the mixture from time to time.

Boil the duck in masses of water with the bay leaves and enough onion and lemon to give the water a good strong flavour: it should be tender and not overcooked. Serve hot with the vegetables described above, or cold with a rather special salad. Welsh Salt Duck would also be marvellous in an out-of-the-ordinary picnic.

TOAD-IN-THE-HOLE

Serves 2

2 lamb loin chops

2 beef sausages

2 lamb's kidneys

2 rashers of bacon

2 eggs, separated

½ pint (300 ml) milk

4 oz (100 g) plain flour

salt and pepper

Oven temperatures:
Gas Mark 4/350°F/180°C
Gas Mark 7/425°F/220°C

No wonder Toad-in-the-hole has such a bad reputation: sausages and batter are not really Toad-in-the-hole. It is, in fact, a very old and traditional way of turning leftover meat into a filling hot meal. Strictly speaking it should be made with leftover beef or steak, but, believe me, there is nothing that could not go into a Toad-in-the-hole, cooked or uncooked, that wouldn't taste good. In this recipe I've used a Sainsbury's pre-packed mixed grill as the base, but if you wish to use other toads, the choice is yours. Both toads and holes go well with buttered cabbage.

Preheat the oven to lower setting. Arrange the chops, sausages, kidneys and bacon symmetrically in a shallow baking dish. Season. Bake in the preheated oven for 12 minutes; then increase the temperature to the higher setting and leave for a further 5 minutes.

Meanwhile, make the batter by beating together the egg yolks, the milk and the flour to produce a smooth mixture. Just before you are ready to add the batter to the meat, whip the egg whites until they peak (but before they become dry) and fold them into the batter. After 5 minutes at the higher temperature, remove the meat from the oven, swiftly add the batter and return to the oven for a further 20 minutes.

BUBBLE AND SQUEAK

1½ lb (675 g) salt beef, cooked and sliced thinly

6 oz (175 g) butter

1½ lb (675 g) cabbage, cooked and sliced small

salt and pepper

'What mortals call Bubble and Squeak
When midst the Fry-ing Pan in accents savage
The Beef so surly quarrels with the Cabbage.'

This little ditty dating from 1795 not only illustrates what an old English dish Bubble and Squeak is, but also two other interesting facts: that the name refers to the noise it is thought to make as it cooks, and that Bubble and Squeak proper is not a fry-up of leftover potatoes, cabbage and onion, but a dish of fried boiled beef and cabbage.

The early nineteenth century cookery writers took Bubble and Squeak very seriously, specifying salt beef, boiled and a little underdone if possible, and that the beef and cabbage should be only lightly fried and seasoned with plenty of pepper.

Leftover cooked cabbage, cold cooked potatoes and leftover boiled onion all fried in butter or beef dripping is in fact a development of an old Irish Hallowe'en dish called Colcannon. The proportions are two parts of boiled potato to one part each of cabbage and onion. If you wish to make it, mix all together in the frying pan, pressing down hard until brown; then turn them over and repeat on the other side. The original Irish dish was baked, with a pool of butter in the centre.

Sauté the meat gently for a few minutes in half the butter; then sprinkle with a little salt and plenty of pepper. Put in a serving dish. Fry the cabbage in the remaining butter for a few more minutes. Season and pile on to the meat.

Serve with pickled cucumbers or walnuts, or a melted butter sauce flavoured with mustard. Equally authentic, though a little reminiscent of the fish-and-chip shop, is to give this dish a simple sprinkling of vinegar.

Cornish Pasties
Bubble and Squeak with mustard and butter sauce

CORNISH PASTIES

1 lb (450 g) shortcrust
pastry, made with lard

1 lb (450 g) pie beef: rump
or chuck steak, or skirt

4 oz (100 g) onions,
chopped finely

3 oz (75 g) yellow swede,
flaked

8 oz (225 g) potato, flaked

salt and pepper

1 egg, beaten, to glaze

Oven temperatures:
Gas Mark 6/400°F/200°C
Gas Mark 4/350°F/180°C

*A true Cornish pasty is both an excellent example of
fine British regional cookery, and a delicious dish in its
own right. This version will show you just what
you've been missing all these years. Traditionally,
minced beef and carrots were not used for the filling;
and the swede and potato were scraped into flakes
rather than sliced.*

Preheat the oven to the higher setting. Roll out
your pastry and cut it into four discs, using side
plates as markers for the shape. Chill while you
prepare the filling.

Cut away all the skin and gristle from the
meat; then chop it roughly or slice into thin
flakes. Season. Take the filling ingredients and
place in layers on one side of each pastry disc.
Brush the edges with beaten egg, fold the other
half of the pastry disc over the filling to give it a
half-moon shape and twist the edges or pinch
them together to seal the pastry and give it its
characteristic rope-like, zig-zag finish. It is also
traditional to mark initials in the corner of each,
though this is only strictly necessary if the
fillings have been varied to cater for individual
tastes. (For instance, mine are always made
without onion.) Make two small steam holes in
the top of each pasty and brush with the rest of
the egg glaze. Bake in the preheated oven for
10 minutes; then at the lower setting for a further
40 minutes. Cover, if they seem to you to be
browning too fast.

FRUIT-STUFFED SHOULDER OF LAMB

Serves 6

1 shoulder of lamb, weighing about 3½ lb (1.6 kg)

4 oz (100 g) mixed dried peaches and apricots, sliced

4 dessertspoons (4 × 10 ml spoon) lemon juice

1 heaped teaspoon (1–2 × 5 ml spoon) dried mint

2 cloves of garlic, crushed

1 lb (450 g) onions, unpeeled and quartered

4 bay leaves

12 black peppercorns

12 allspice berries

2 oz (50 g) lemon peel, cut into strips

1 heaped teaspoon (1–2 × 5 ml spoon) salt

1 oz (25 g) parsley

In Victorian times the forequarters of sheep were considered far tastier than the rear legs, and both were often boiled. This boned and boiled shoulder is as sweet and tender as could be, and is flavoured with mint and apricot – a combination from the Eastern Mediterranean, brought back to us by the Crusaders.

First, remove the shoulder blade from the lamb by cutting carefully down either side of the bone, being careful not to break through the skin, until you reach the joint. Use the tip of your knife to cut through the joint and remove the blade bone. Enlarge the pocket down to the remaining bone.

Prepare the stuffing by tossing the sliced dried fruit in the lemon juice and mixing it with the mint and crushed garlic. Stuff the lamb with this mixture and cobble together with toothpicks, or sew it up.

Fill a saucepan (large enough to accommodate the lamb) three-quarters full with water. Add the quartered onions, bay leaves, peppercorns, allspice berries, lemon peel, salt and the parsley to the water; then bring to the boil. Allow to simmer for 5 minutes before putting in the lamb, knuckle side down. Add the shoulder blade. From the time the liquid comes to the boil, simmer for 15 minutes per pound (450 g), plus 10 extra minutes. Turn the shoulder over half-way through the cooking period. To serve cold, cool in the liquid. To serve hot, remove from the liquid, leave to stand for 15 minutes, then slice thinly and pour on a little of the cooking liquid. (The remaining stock is marvellous for soups, especially for the Barley Broth on page 7.)

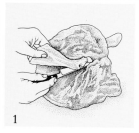

1

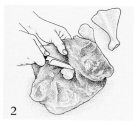

2

KEDGEREE

4 lb (1.8 kg) smoked haddock (Finnan is suitable)

2 bay leaves

1 lb (450 g) basmati or other long grain rice

8 oz (225 g) butter

8 eggs, hard-boiled

2 teaspoons (2 × 5 ml spoon) ground cumin

1 teaspoon (5 ml spoon) ground coriander

1 teaspoon (5 ml spoon) turmeric

This is one of the few dishes derived from our Indian connection that the British haven't made spicier. Generally kedgeree in this country has no spices in it at all – yet in other Commonwealth countries, such as Australia and New Zealand (where many members of the Indian army retired), kedgeree is always served with a light curried flavour. It has been known in this country in various forms since the mid-eighteenth century, and is a true Anglo-Indian dish: a product of both culinary traditions, previously existing – in this form – in neither. It is a marvellous breakfast or supper dish, is exceedingly good at lunchtimes, is just the thing for high tea and it makes a satisfyingly simple dinner.

Cover the fish with cold water, throw in the bay leaves and heat gently until the water is just beginning to boil. The fish is now cooked, so turn off the heat. Remove the fish, but do not throw away the water.

Melt 1 oz (25 g) of the butter in a large saucepan with a close-fitting lid, add the rice and turn around until evenly coated and opaque. Then add twice the volume of the rice in liquid, using the water in which the fish was cooked. (To check the volume of the rice simply pour it into a jug. The level it reaches is the level to which you fill the same container twice with liquid.) Bring the rice to the boil, without the lid, and then simmer until the level of water has fallen below the level of rice (you will see holes appear in the surface of the rice). Do not stir at any point. Take the rice off the heat, cover with a tea–towel and press the saucepan lid tightly home. Leave undisturbed for at least 15 minutes over the lowest possible plate or gas flame, using a diffuser if available. When the time is up, remove the towel and lid and gently fluff up the rice with a wooden spoon. If by any chance some of the rice is sticky, put it in a colander over boiling water and cover with a cloth and lid for about 10 minutes.

While the rice cooks, flake the fish into largish pieces and remove every scrap of skin and bone. Shell the eggs and chop them roughly.

When the rice is ready, melt the rest of the butter and gently cook the spices for 2–3 minutes. Stir in the rice immediately: if it is allowed to cool, it will begin to congeal. (If you need to keep it warm, keep it in a colander over boiling water, as described above.) When the rice, butter and spices are perfectly blended, stir in the eggs and then the fish, with as light a touch as possible. Turn into a warmed ovenproof dish and serve immediately, or put in the oven to keep warm or to reheat later.

KIPPERS

Serves 2

2 whole kippers

2 pints (1.2 litres) water

A hundred years ago, a light supper of kippers was a very different kettle of fish to what it is nowadays, for then it meant smoked salmon. The salmon were caught, split, gutted, salted and smoked – or, in a word, kippered – after they had spawned: 'to kipper' meant to spawn or hatch. The kippered herring that we eat is a nineteenth century invention: herrings were then so cheap and plentiful (even in 1928, you could still buy a stone of them for a penny), any means of preserving them was welcome – and this, of course, is a particularly tasty means. Look for as light and golden a cure as possible. Kippers are at their best in summer.

Boil the water. Put the kippers skin side up in a large frying pan. Pour enough boiling water over them to cover. If they have come straight from the fridge, simmer the kippers for 1 minute on a medium heat; then turn the heat off and leave them for 5 minutes. If they have not come straight from the fridge, simply leave them for 5 minutes. They will then be ready to eat; moist and delicious. And the house won't stink for hours! Many people would serve them with a poached egg on top.

45

BRAISED BABY TURKEY WITH CUCUMBER AND ARTICHOKE

Serves 6–8

1 prepared baby turkey or large chicken, weighing 5 lb (2.2 kg) when dressed

1 oz (25 g) beef dripping

1 tablespoon (15 ml spoon) plain flour

¼ pint (150 ml) water

¼ pint (150 ml) wine

2 anchovy fillets

1 medium-size onion

8 cloves

6 oz (175 g) fatty streaky bacon

1 cucumber, about 9 inches (23 cm) long

6–8 oz (175–225 g) artichoke bottoms, canned or fresh, sliced in half

lemon juice, to taste

This is another recipe from Fletcher Christian's grandmother's cookbook. Baby turkeys are available in the shops at non-seasonal times, but a large chicken would be just fine. This recipe has a lovely, old-fashioned farmyard flavour that even the most hardened city dweller will melt for.

Press down on to the turkey or chicken breastbone to snap its rib cage, and flatten the bird as much as possible. Remove any excess fat and the parson's nose.

In a heavy saucepan, just big enough to hold the bird, melt the beef dripping. Brown any giblets well, then remove. Put the turkey in the pan, breast side down, and cook until golden. Turn it over and repeat. Remove the bird. Stir in the flour and keep stirring until it is a nice rich brown.

Add the water and wine together and stir until well mixed and simmering. Add the anchovies. Return the turkey or chicken to the saucepan, breast side up, and put any giblets (but not the liver) and the onion (cut in half and spiked with the cloves) around the bird. Lay the strips of bacon across the bird's breast. Cover and cook gently on top of the stove for 15 minutes per pound (450 g), plus an extra 15 minutes.

Cut the cucumber in half down the middle, remove the seeds and cut into ¼ inch (5 mm) thick segments. Blanch for a few moments in boiling water. Slice the liver.

When the turkey or chicken is cooked, move it on to a warm plate: it will stay warm for half an hour. Strain the cooking liquid into another saucepan and reduce it over the heat to a single cream consistency. Add the sliced artichoke, the cucumber and the sliced liver. Sharpen the sauce with a little lemon juice. Slice the bird, and serve it with the sauce.

MACKEREL WITH RHUBARB AND MINT SAUCE

4 mackerel, weighing about 12 oz–1 lb (350–450 g) each

2 teaspoons (2 × 5 ml spoon) salt

1 teaspoon (5 ml spoon) pepper

½ lemon, sliced, plus its rind, grated

4–5 teaspoons (4–5 × 5 ml spoon) dried mint

4 oz (100 g) onions, sliced

6 fl oz (175 ml) water

1 lb (450 g) rhubarb, cut into 1-inch (2.5 cm) lengths

1 clove of garlic, crushed

3 heaped dessertspoons (4–6 × 10 ml spoon) sugar

salt and pepper (optional)

To garnish:

fresh mint

Oven temperature:
Gas Mark 4/350°F/180°C

Mackerel are at their best in April, May and June: in fact the Scandinavians specially celebrate their first catch of May mackerel which is said to have the mildness and delicacy of trout. So try to eat fresh mackerel at this time, and smoked mackerel not long afterwards. Being an oily fish, it needs a sour sauce: gooseberries are a classic British accompaniment, but here I have used rhubarb, which is as sharp as gooseberries and much prettier.

Fillet and gut the mackerel by cutting down through their bodies either side of the backbone, starting behind the head and finishing near the tail. (Reserve the backbones, but throw away the guts.) Snip the bone at each end with scissors, but leave the heads and tails intact and attached to the bodies. Rub their flesh with a mixture of the salt, pepper, grated lemon rind and 3 teaspoons (3 × 5 ml spoon) of the dried mint.

Preheat the oven. Place the 4 backbones in a large baking dish. On top of these strew the sliced onion and sliced lemon and sprinkle on the final 1–2 teaspoons (1–2 × 5 ml spoon) dried mint. Lay each mackerel on top of its backbone. Pour in the water, cover tightly with foil and bake in the preheated oven for 30–40 minutes, or until just done. Drain off the cooking juice and return the fish, covered, to the oven, which should be held at the lowest possible temperature to keep the fish warm while the sauce is being prepared.

Rapidly reduce the fish stock by boiling, to about 3 tablespoons (3 × 15 ml spoon). Add the rhubarb and the garlic and simmer until the rhubarb has lost its shape. Liquidise with its juice and sieve. Add the sugar to the sauce; then taste and season if necessary. Pour on a plate and place the mackerel (which may be skinned if you wish) on top. Garnish with fresh mint.

EIGHTEENTH CENTURY CHICKEN WITH SWEETBREADS, WILD MUSHROOMS AND BACON

Serves 4

1 corn-fed chicken,
weighing about 3 lb
(1.3 kg)

4 oz (100 g) onions

½ lemon

1 carrot

2 bay leaves

½–¾ oz (15–20 g) dried
wild or cultivated
mushrooms

1 lb (450 g) lamb's
sweetbreads

4 oz (100 g) lean bacon,
chopped small

½ teaspoon (2.5 ml spoon)
ground mace, plus a little
extra

¼ teaspoon (1.25 ml
spoon) ground nutmeg, plus
a little extra

a little butter

¼ pint (150 ml) double
cream

a little lemon juice

salt and black pepper

When I first discovered this recipe in the kitchen book of Fletcher Christian's grandmother, it was simply called 'To Stue a chicken', and thinking it rather ordinary-sounding, I ignored it. It took me five more years to discover it to be one of the most luxurious ways to enjoy chicken I've ever tasted. I recommend that you start preparations the day before you intend to eat this dish, in order to avoid last minute panics.

Bone the chicken, either by leaving the skin intact or by slicing along the side: first remove the wishbone, then run a knife along either side of the rib cage towards the parson's nose. Dislocate the joints and remove. Leave the wings intact, but cut out the thigh bone of each leg. Discard as much fat as you can. Put the bones in 1½ pints (900 ml) water and add the onion, half-lemon, carrot and bay leaves; then simmer uncovered until reduced to just ½ pint (300 ml) of stock. Strain and leave overnight to cool.

Put the mushrooms in ½ pint (300 ml) water and simmer very, very gently until they are reconstituted and tender, and there is very little liquid left – though add a little more water if you need to, to avoid burning. Leave in their liquid overnight. Soak the sweetbreads in slightly salted cold water for at least 4 hours, changing the water often. Again, it is better to start in the evening.

When you are ready to assemble the chicken, skim the fat from the stock, heat it to boiling point and then plunge in the drained sweetbreads for 5 minutes. Remove and plunge into cold water. Once firm, pick off the globules of fat or any really thick membrane, but do not remove it all as it helps them keep their shape.

Take the mushrooms from their liquid and add that to the stock as well. Reserve 6 sweetbreads and some nice-looking mushrooms, then mix the remainder together with the chopped bacon. Add the mace and nutmeg and lots of black pepper and a little salt, tossing well. Fill the chicken with this mixture, and either sew or fasten together with toothpicks. If you are using toothpicks, try and point them across the chicken rather than along, as this will make carving easier.

Melt enough butter to cover the bottom of a wide saucepan, then gently brown both sides of the chicken, taking great care not to tear it when turning. Clean out the pan, add the stock (which should be just over ½ pint/300 ml) and once that is boiling add the chicken, breast side up. Cover the pan with its lid and cook for 50–60 minutes.

Transfer the chicken to a warmed plate, turn up the heat under the pan to reduce the juices a little and then add the cream. When you have the texture you desire, add the reserved mushrooms and sweetbreads and the extra spices. Remove the wings and the remaining leg joints, then slice across the chicken. Place a little of the sauce on each plate and place a thick slice of chicken in the middle. Sprinkle each serving with a little lemon juice: guests tend to overdo it if you give them lemon wedges!

SWEET COURSES

EGG CUSTARD

3 oz (75 g) granulated sugar

5 egg yolks

1 teaspoon (5 ml spoon) cornflour (optional)

¾ pint (450 ml) milk

1 teaspoon (5 ml spoon) vanilla essence, or any other flavouring (see method)

1–2 tablespoons (1–2 × 15 ml spoon) unsalted butter, softened (optional)

Egg custard – sweetened milk thickened with egg – may not be easy to make, but the result is superb and well worth the effort. Every British cook should know how to master this sauce, which the French pay the tribute of calling crème Anglaise.

Gradually beat the sugar into the egg yolks and continue beating hard for 2–3 minutes, until the mixture has turned a pale yellow and, when you lift a little of the mixture out and let it drop across the rest, it will form a slowly–dissolving ribbon on the surface. (See the diagram.) Beat in the cornflour, if you wish to use it (it acts as a minor safety net, allowing you to heat the custard a little more than you would otherwise be able to). Heat the milk in a pan to boiling, and pour it on to the egg yolks in a thin stream, while continuing to beat the egg yolk mixture.

Pour the mixture into a saucepan and heat gently, stirring continually with a wooden spatula or spoon, making sure that you reach into every corner of the saucepan. When the sauce coats the spoon with a light, creamy layer, it is done (165°F/75°C). This will be nowhere near simmering point, and may seem barely warm to you. However, take immediately off the heat and continue beating for a minute or two to cool the sauce slightly. Strain it through a fine sieve, and flavour as you wish: 1 teaspoon (5 ml spoon) vanilla essence for 'classic' custard, or 1 tablespoon (15 ml spoon) of rum, brandy, strong coffee, orange flower water or rose water . . . (by the way, a rum–flavoured, proper egg custard is the perfect accompaniment – as well as the most traditional – for Christmas pudding). If you have to keep the custard warm before serving, leave it in a bowl over a saucepan of warm water. For extra richness, beat in the softened unsalted butter at the last minute.

BAKED PIPPINS WITH BAY CUSTARD

4 Cox's orange pippins, weighing about 8 oz (225 g) each

2 oz (50 g) butter, softened

1 oz (25 g) raisins

1 oz (25 g) sultanas

½ oz (15 g) muscovado sugar

1 teaspoon (5 ml spoon) cinnamon

¼ pint (150 ml) cider or water

For the custard:

2 eggs, separated

2 tablespoons (2 × 15 ml spoon) cornflour

1 pint (600 ml) milk

4 fresh bay leaves

Oven temperature:
Gas Mark 4/350°F/180°C

Cox's orange pippins are excellent cookers, needing virtually no sugar. As well as making a memorable pie filling, they are perfect bakers and their perfumed pulp is a delightful change from the sharp Bramley. Here they are served with an unusual foamy custard flavoured with bay leaf – a simple country idea we should never have stopped using.

Preheat the oven. Core the apples. Mix together the butter, raisins, sultanas, sugar and cinnamon. Stuff the cored apples with this mixture, and put them in a baking dish. Scatter any leftover stuffing mixture on the bottom of the dish. Score each apple around its equator, and then make four cuts, in the shape of a cross, from the top of each apple down to the middle cut: this will enable the apple to open up as it bakes. Pour in the cider or water and bake in the preheated oven, uncovered, for 35 minutes or so.

Towards the end of the baking, make the custard. Whisk the egg yolks and cornflour together with a little of the milk. Flavour the remaining milk by heating it with the bay leaves. Take out the leaves and pour the milk over the egg mixture, stirring all the time. Return the custard to the pan and stir over a low heat until it boils and thickens. Leave to cool slightly. Whisk the egg whites until stiff and then fold into the custard.

You serve this old-fashioned pudding the new-fashioned way. Quickly remove the top half of the skins of the cooked apples. Place each in the centre of a fairly large, flat plate. Pour the custard around each apple – not over it. Reduce and dribble the cooking liquid from the baking pan over the exposed apple flesh and, if you like, pour more over the custard, perhaps making a pattern as you do so.

QUEEN OF PUDDINGS

1 pint (600 ml) milk

rind of ½ lemon, grated

4 oz (100 g) fresh white breadcrumbs

2 oz (50 g) butter, cut into small pieces, plus extra for greasing

2 oz (50 g) caster sugar

2 eggs, separated

3 heaped tablespoons (4–5 × 15 ml spoon) sharp red jam or jelly

1½ teaspoons (3 × 2.5 ml spoon) lemon juice

Oven temperatures
Gas Mark 4/350°F/180°C
Gas Mark 6/400°F/200°C

The use of leftover bread for sweet dishes is very old, and British cuisine has preserved this better than most. (The original meaning of biscuit, for example, was bread 'bis cuit' (twice cooked), giving one of those primeval biscuits, rusks.) In addition to the famous bread and butter pudding, we have apple charlotte, queen of puddings, poor knights of Windsor, summer pudding and brown bread ice cream, to name but a few. One of the reasons, perhaps, that bread is used so frequently in British puddings is that it acts as a perfect vehicle for soaking up the juices of our envied apples and summer soft fruits.

Put the milk in a saucepan with the lemon zest, and bring slowly to the boil. Turn off, and leave to steep for 15 minutes.

Preheat the oven to the first setting. Put the breadcrumbs, the pieces of butter and half the caster sugar in a bowl. Pour on the hot milk through a sieve. Mix together, cover, and leave for 10 minutes. Then beat together the egg yolks and add them to the mixture. Pour into a buttered ovenproof dish and bake in the preheated oven for 40 minutes.

Meanwhile, mix the jam or jelly with the lemon juice, to form a runnier texture than normal. Whip the egg whites until they begin to form soft peaks and add half the remaining sugar. Whip again, add the last of the sugar, and whip for a final time.

Remove the pudding from the oven and raise the temperature to the higher setting. Spread the pudding with the jam and lemon juice, and then smooth on the meringue. Finish off with a pretty pattern made with the back of a fork. Return to the oven for 5–8 minutes, until the meringue is lightly browned. Allow to cool a little before serving (about 10 minutes).

Although not traditional, this dish is delicious made with apricot jam, thinned with brandy or rum.

Cherry Layer Pudding
Queen of Puddings ▶

CHERRY LAYER PUDDING

Serves 4–6

8 oz (225 g) sugar

¼ pint (150 ml) white wine

1¼ lb (550 g) pitted cherries

5 oz (150 g) butter

2 eggs, separated

a generous pinch of ground cinnamon

5 oz (150 g) fresh white breadcrumbs

4 tablespoons (4 × 15 ml spoon) milk

Oven temperature:
Gas Mark 7/425°F/220°C

Cherries are the pride of Kent and are used in as many ways as there are cherry trees – steamed in puddings, baked in batters, simmered in syrups. This is another pudding that uses breadcrumbs and which allows great individual expression. Choose the sharper red cherries if you have the choice.

Cook 3 oz (75 g) of the sugar and the white wine together, to make a syrup. Add the cherries and poach for a few minutes until the syrup is coloured and flavoured. Drain the cherries, reserving the syrup.

Preheat the oven. Cream together the butter and the remaining sugar. Beat the egg yolks and add with the cinnamon. Stir in the breadcrumbs and the milk. Lastly, beat the egg whites until stiff and fold into the mixture as lightly and swiftly as possible. Layer this mixture with the cherries in a greased, shallow pie dish (starting with a cherry layer), and bake in the preheated oven for half an hour. Turn out, and serve with the reheated syrup and some cream.

Some delicious variations can be made by altering the flavourings slightly to suit your taste. For example, try flavouring the mixture with orange or lemon rind, or the syrup with rum or brandy. For a delectably rich syrup, use port or a good sweet oloroso sherry instead of the white wine.

KENTISH FRUIT CREAM

Serves 6–8

1 lb (450 g) mixed summer fruits (e.g., cherries, red and white currants, raspberries and strawberries)

1 lb (450 g) preserving or granulated sugar

1 pint (600 ml) double cream

Keeping the softest summer fruits, such as the raspberries and strawberries, to one side, boil the summer fruits with the preserving sugar for 10 minutes. Add the softer fruit to the pan and cook for another 2 minutes. Sieve and cool the fruit mixture. When cool, stir in the double cream and whisk up the whole lot together until thickened.

CREAMS, WHIPS AND FOOLS

Serves 4–6

There are many terms to describe our delicious fruit desserts, but no one term seems to have a meaning exclusive of any other, and there are no precise rules as to exactly what constitutes, say, a fool. With a basic guide-line of 1 lb (450 g) crushed fruit to ½ pint (300 ml) double cream, or proper custard, or half and half, the freedom of the fruit orchard is yours. Serving quantities are really only a guideline, and, with today's ideas on healthy eating, these creamy desserts tend to be served more as accompaniments to fresh fruit, making them go even further. Further refinements include the very British incorporation of cake or biscuit into the mixture – in particular, almond-based biscuits; the use of fruit juices instead of fruit pulp and the inclusion of grated peel and alcohol in the finished dish.

BOODLE'S ORANGE FOOL

Serves 6–8

thin strips of sponge

grated rind and juice of 2 lemons

grated rind and juice of 4 oranges

3 oz (75 g) caster sugar

1 pint (600 ml) double cream, whipped softly

Line a deep serving dish with the thin strips of sponge. Mix together the grated rind and juice of the lemons and oranges with the caster sugar and stir until dissolved.

Thoroughly incorporate into the mixture ½ pint (300 ml) of the softly whipped cream, and pour the whole into the sponge lining. Chill for several hours. Serve with the remaining ½ pint (300 ml) whipped cream piped on the top.

EDINBURGH FOG

Serves 6–8

1 pint (600 ml) double cream

1 tablespoon (15 ml spoon) caster sugar

1 teaspoon (5 ml spoon) vanilla essence

4 oz (100 g) ratafia biscuits, crushed

2 oz (50 g) almonds, blanched and chopped

Simply whip up the cream with the caster sugar and vanilla essence. Stir in the crushed biscuits and chopped almonds and chill well before serving.

MIXED FRUIT PIE

8 oz (225 g) mixed dried
fruits (apricots, peaches,
apples, prunes, etc.)

just under ½ pint (300 ml)
orange juice

1 tablespoon (15 ml spoon)
lemon juice

1 oz (25 g) butter, plus
extra for greasing

1 lb (450 g) cooking apples

2–3 dessertspoons (2–3 ×
10 ml spoon) granulated
sugar

2 teaspoons (2 × 5 ml
spoon) orange flower water

2 teaspoons (2 × 5 ml
spoon) rose water

1 heaped teaspoon (1–2 ×
5 ml spoon) cinnamon

1 lb (450 g) puff pastry

half a beaten egg

Oven temperatures:
Gas Mark 7/425°F/220°C
Gas Mark 4/350°F/180°C

Dried fruits, oranges and spices came to Britain with the returning Crusaders. This pie delectably combines these with flower waters, to make a pie that is both absolutely British and very Arabic – in the time of Richard II there was virtually no difference between the two cuisines.

Gently simmer the dried fruits together with the orange and lemon juices and the butter, until most of the liquid has been absorbed. Meanwhile, peel and core the apples and cut them into eighths. Toss them in the granulated sugar, and mix in with the now plump and cooked dried fruits. Add the orange flower and rose waters and the cinnamon. Leave to cool a little.

Preheat the oven to the higher temperature. Take an 8-inch × 1-inch (20 × 2.5 cm) pie or flan dish, and use rather over half the pastry to line its bottom. Fill with the mixed fruit mixture. Paint around the outside seam with water, and roll out and cover the pie with the other half of the pastry. Mark the pie edges, and cut air vents in the top of the pastry. Decorate with cut-out pastry leaves, and glaze very lightly with the beaten half-egg, mixed with a little water. Bake in the preheated oven for 20 minutes, and then at the lower oven temperature for a further 20 minutes. Serve warm rather than hot.

Mixed Fruit Pie
Pineapple and Mincemeat Pie

PINEAPPLE AND MINCEMEAT PIE

Serves 4–6

1½ lb (675 g) fresh
pineapple, peeled, sliced
and segmented into eighths

2 oz (50 g) demerara sugar
(optional)

1 lb (450 g) shortcrust
pastry

8 oz (225 g) fruit
mincemeat

a scant ½ teaspoon (2.5 ml
spoon) ground ginger

1 egg, beaten, to glaze

Oven temperatures:
Gas Mark 7/425°F/220°C
Gas Mark 4/350°F/180°C

*Pineapples, native to South America, were first
mentioned in this country as having been presented to
Oliver Cromwell, and they were afterwards regarded
as a great delicacy by Charles II. The wonderful
shape of the pineapple is formed by the tiny fruits of all
the flowers gradually fusing into one. You often see
the shape used decoratively or monumentally: the
pineapple was regarded as a symbol of hospitality
during the great country house era.*

Preheat the oven to the higher temperature.
Sprinkle the pineapple segments with the
demerara sugar, if you wish. Roll out just over
half of the shortcrust pastry, and put it in a
9-inch (23 cm) pie dish. Put the mincemeat on
the bottom and cover with the pineapple
segments. Sprinkle with the ginger. Roll out the
rest of the pastry; then cover and decorate the pie
with pastry pineapples. Glaze with the beaten
egg. Bake for 20 minutes, and then for another
15–20 minutes at the lower oven temperature.

BRAMLEY AND MARMALADE TART

Serves 6–8

10 oz (275 g) wholemeal or
other pastry

1 egg, separated

2 generous tablespoons (2–3
× 15 ml spoon) sharp
chunky marmalade

12 oz (350 g) Bramley
apples, peeled, cored and
sliced

2 × 5.29 oz (150 g) carton
of natural yogurt

1 oz (25 g) walnut pieces

*The Bramley apple is so British, it won't even grow
in other countries! Although you can cook with any
apple, including Cox's Orange Pippins, the sharpness
of Bramleys naturally works specially well with
marmalade, another most British product, especially if
it is a dark, thick, chunky version. The thin, sweet
versions won't end up as tasty, though. This recipe
was developed by Andrew Foss of East Bridgford,
Notts., when he was only 14, and it won him a prize
in a national competition.*

Preheat the oven. Roll out the pastry to fit a
7-inch (18 cm) flan dish and bake it blind.
Immediately you take it from the oven, paint the
pastry with the lightly beaten egg white then

return to the oven for a brief time to ensure the egg white is set and has sealed the pastry.

Mix the marmalade and the egg yolk together, then stir in the sliced apples and pile the mixture neatly and evenly into the pastry base.

Bake for 30 minutes, or until the apples have sunk a little and are tipped with brown. Don't worry if there is a syrup forming.

While the flan is baking, carefully tip the yogurt into a very fine sieve and let it drain. If you stir it more than enough just to break it up gently you will thin the yogurt.

Remove the cooked flan from the oven and let it cool for 10–15 minutes until just lukewarm. Spread the drained yogurt evenly over the pie, sprinkle on the walnuts and serve at once. The flan is also excellent served cold.

SYLLABUKS

Serves 8–10

½ pint (300 ml) wine, or
¼ pint (150 ml) wine and
¼ pint (150 ml) fruit pulp
(to make a fruit syllabub)

6 oz (175 g) caster sugar

grated rind and juice of
2 lemons (optional)

1½ pints (900 ml) double
cream

These are different in essence from creams and fools. They were originally extremely theatrical to serve, but since the demise of the family cow they have become less so. We can now no longer produce the rich froth on the top by milking our cow directly into a bowl of sweet wine, but have to content ourselves with the more mundane whisk. Do remember, though, that these dishes of cream and wine – and fruit, in the case of fruit syllabubs – may separate, rather in the way of Irish coffee (in fact they are often served, like Irish coffee, in glasses).

Mix all the ingredients except the cream together, including the lemon rind and juice if you want to sharpen the flavour. Leave to marinate for 4 hours or overnight in a refrigerator. Liquidise or force through a sieve if using fruit pulp, and whip in the cream to form soft peaks. Pour into glasses and chill before serving.

RASPBERRY SYLLABUB

8 oz (225 g) raspberries

¼ pint (150 ml) Amontillado or other dry sherry, or dry white wine

2 tablespoons (2 × 15 ml spoon) brandy

grated rind of 1 orange

grated rind of ½ lemon

3 oz (75 g) sugar

¾ pint (450 ml) double cream

The delightful colour and sharp richness of this fruit syllabub are the epitome of everything best about British desserts. Keep some of the fruit back for garnishing and always serve this syllabub after a relatively light meal. Some brandy, especially a raspberry-flavoured one (page 92), dribbled over the fruit in the glass is excellent.

Keep 1–3 raspberries per serving to one side. Crush the remainder slightly and then put them in a bowl with all the other ingredients, except the cream. (If you have no Amontillado, and use dry sherry or dry white wine instead, you might like to add a little extra sugar.) Leave to marinate for at least 4 hours in a warm place, or overnight in a refrigerator.

Force the mixture through a sieve. Pour in the cream and then whip to soft peaks. Put the reserved fruit in the bottom of your serving glasses and top with the syllabub. Chill well before serving, perhaps with unfilled brandy snaps. This style of syllabub may not separate but do not worry if it does.

In keeping with British traditions, this wondrous mixture is perfect for mixing with crushed meringues, with or without more raspberries; for making cake-structured puddings, such as a raspberry flavoured Boodle's (see page 55); or for topping a trifle. Imagine making a trifle with squares of madeira cake, raspberry jam, fresh raspberries and a raspberry syllabub!

Raspberry Syllabub

Trifle

mley and
rmalade
t

61

LONDON SYLLABUB

½ pint (300 ml) port

6 oz (175 g) caster sugar

a little grated nutmeg

1½ pints (900 ml) double cream

Mix the port, caster sugar and nutmeg together. Add the cream and whip to soft peaks. Pour into glasses and chill before serving.

THE TRIFLE

Is anything more evocative than a trifle, or more discussed? Yet is there an absolutely basic, traditional recipe? The answer, surprisingly, is no. Once, a trifle was simply a pudding made of layers and covered with jellies, creams and custards. Mrs Beeton regularly gave recipes for what she called an Indian trifle, based on cutting cold rice-flour custard into shapes and piling these into a decorated tower, covered and stuffed with as many colourful ingredients as you or your cook could get. Others were topped with High Whips, an extravagant version of syllabub rather similar to the raspberry one on page 60.

Since then, we have come to a certain agreement about what we expect a trifle to be. It is layered and in a glass bowl. The bottom layer is of sponge squares, split and smeared generously with strawberry or raspberry jam. A sliced jam roll is suitable. Once these are arranged in the bottom of the bowl, they are sprinkled lavishly with a sweet sherry or a port – sweet sherry is preferable to dry. In Australasia, and for children, the sponges are held together with a flavoured jelly instead of alcohol.

The next layer is traditionally fruit. Any fresh fruit is good, even orange segments, but tropical delights, such as kiwifruit, mango and passion fruit, are best if you cannot get summer soft fruits. Custard is the next layer: this can be custard made with powder, but egg custard would be more authentic if you are good at making it. Flavour it well with the old-fashioned favourites, such as coconut, orange flower water or grated orange rind.

Whipped cream is the inescapable topping, often studded with toasted almonds and cherries.

The proportion of any one layer to another is absolutely up to you, but be generous, make it long enough in advance to exchange flavours properly and serve it really cold. Trifle is best the next day, but don't put the cream on until the last minute.

Now, once you know that almost anything layered can be properly called a trifle, there's no need to stick to the basic recipe at all. Here are a few interesting ideas:

- Layer the sponges with lemon or orange curd; dribble on sherry, brandy or Calvados; use stewed apples flavoured with orange or lemon and top with citrus-flavoured custard.
- Use apricot or peach jam; brandy, sherry or apricot brandy; fresh peaches or apricots sprinkled with toasted hazelnuts, and an almond or brandy-flavoured custard.
- Spread the sponges with crushed fresh blackberries; sprinkle with gin or brandy; layer with stewed apples or more summer soft fruits, and top with a raspberry or blackberry syllabub.
- Use cherry jam, fresh cherries and rum or cherry brandy; use crushed pineapple, fresh pineapple, lime juice and gin or rum; use chocolate sponge, fresh raspberries, brandy and cream flavoured with rosewater . . . in fact, use anything you like that is high quality, fresh, colourful and seasonal.

8 oz (200 g) dried apricots, halved if large

4 oz (100 g) prunes, stoned and halved if large

4 oz (100 g) figs

4 oz (100 g) dates

4 oz (100 g) large seedless raisins

1 oz (25 g) currants

1 oz (25 g) chopped peel or glacé cherries

thinly peeled rind and juice of 1 medium-size lemon

1 stick of cinnamon

70 cl bottle of port or Rich Ruby wine

up to ¼ pint (150 ml) dark rum

2 sachets of powdered gelatine

In Australasia, Christmas time coincides with summer. Most families struggle with traditional British foods, but some make deliciously refreshing puddings like this to replace a steamed one. Entirely in keeping with Christmas traditions in its use of dried fruit and spices, which are so important in our culinary heritage, this shows how flexibly British cooking has adapted to suit the demands of changing climates and ways of eating. Like steamed fruit puddings this matures on keeping for anything up to 7 days if your refrigerator is really cold.

Assemble your dried fruits. The proportions can be varied if you like, but let apricots predominate. Separately, put the raisins, currants, peel or cherries (or a mixture) in a small saucepan together with the thinly peeled rind of the lemon and the cinnamon stick. Add ½ pint (300 ml) of the wine, bring very slowly to the boil, and simmer for 5 minutes. Note that you can substitute cheaper Cyprus ruby wine or British ruby wine with good results.

Make the lemon juice up to ¼ pint (150 ml) with dark rum. Pour this over the first dried fruit mixture. Take the lemon peel from the hot mixture then combine both lots of fruit. Add a further ½ pint (300 ml) of the wine. Cover and leave overnight in a warm but not hot place.

In the morning, drain off the liquid and reserve. Remove the cinnamon stick. Make up the reserved liquid to ¾ pint (450 ml) with wine. If there is a little left over, use it for the next step. Take any leftover wine or a few spoonsful of the liquid from the soaked fruit, and put it into a small saucepan. Sprinkle on the gelatine. Heat very gently until all the grains have melted, but be very wary of burning. Once dissolved, add the ¾ pint (450 ml) of liquid, and stir very well.

Arrange the prepared, mixed dried fruit in a 2½–3-pint (1.5–1.7-litre) pudding basin, perhaps making a pattern on the base with some of the apricots, then putting the remainder on top. Pour in the liquid, shake gently to ensure there are no air bubbles, cover and chill for at least 24 hours.

Plunge the bowl up to its rim in hot water for a few seconds, then put a large plate over the bowl, quickly invert it and turn out the pudding.

You need an exceptionally sharp knife to cut this, or a good serrated-edged knife. You will probably find it best to cut the pudding in half and then to cut neat segments from this.

Serve on flat plates, with a little very cold single or double cream around each portion.

RICE PUDDING

Serves 4

2 oz (50 g) short grain pudding rice

1 pint (600 ml) creamy milk

1 oz (25 g) sugar

1 dessertspoon (10 ml spoon) butter

½ teaspoon (2.5 ml spoon) nutmeg

Oven temperature:
Gas Mark 2/300°F/150°C

Rice first arrived in this country from Spain during Elizabethan times. The sixteenth century herbalist John Gerard tried growing it in his garden, but without much success: agronomists have discovered since that it can grow no further than 45°N, which means that the most northerly rice we know is grown in Hungary and the Camargue.

Best results are obtained from this simple dish by using creamy milk and by using a container only just big enough to hold the uncooked mixture. Cook until the milk level is only just above the rice for the creamiest results: cook longer for a more solid result.

Soak the rice in the cold milk for 2 hours. Then preheat the oven. Put the milk, rice, sugar and butter in a deep 1-pint (600 ml) baking dish. Stir well, sprinkle with the nutmeg and place in the lower half of the preheated oven for 2–2½ hours. Stir every half-hour. Serve.

To make a truly eighteenth century rice pudding, you might try adding to the cooked pudding 4 egg yolks, 2 oz (50 g) dried or crystallised fruit and orange flower water. Then, fold in the 4 beaten egg whites and bake again, perhaps in pastry. This was a favourite of the Hanoverian Georges.

STEAMED PUDDINGS

In Tudor times, sweet puddings were boiled in animal
gut, much as haggis is still. Then the pudding cloth
was developed, and finally the pudding basin, the
pudding itself becoming lighter at every stage.
Whether light or heavy, few other dishes are more
central to our national heritage: say 'pudding'
anywhere in Europe, and everyone will shut their
eyes and think of England!

Here are two basic recipes, followed by six
variants, that will enable you to explore this part of
our national heritage thoroughly. All are designed for
a 1½–2-pint (1–1.2-litre) pudding basin, and should
serve six. Use suet for a heavier result, butter for a
lighter one. I use self-raising flour, which is more to
modern taste.

BASIC RECIPE 1

Serves 6

4oz (100 g) suet or butter
4 oz (100 g) caster sugar
2 eggs, beaten
4 oz (100 g) self-raising flour
1–2 tablespoons (1–2 × 15 ml spoon) cold water
butter for greasing
a pinch of salt

Butter a pudding basin. Cream the suet or butter
and sugar together until fluffy. Add the beaten
eggs, little by little, beating well between each
addition. Sieve the flour and salt together, and
fold in carefully. Add enough water to give a
soft dropping consistency. Spoon in your
flavouring, if one is being used (see under
variations below), and then top with the sponge
mixture. Cover with buttered foil, pleated in the
middle to allow for expansion, and then tie
tightly with string under the rim. Loop the ends
over to form a handle. Stand on a saucer or trivet
in a large saucepan and pour in boiling water,
just up to the bottom of the bowl's rim. Steam
for 1½–2 hours until firm and well risen (if you
have used butter it will need the lesser time; if
suet, the greater), topping up with boiling water
when necessary. Remove from the heat and
leave to shrink slightly before turning out on to a
warmed plate. Serve either with thin custard,
cream, fruit syrups sharpened with lemon juice
or even home–made ice cream.

Fresh breadcrumbs are also commonly used in steamed puddings. Either replace the 4 oz (100 g) flour with 6 oz (175 g) breadcrumbs, or use a mixture of 2 oz (50 g) flour and 2–3 oz (50–75 g) breadcrumbs. Use the same method as for Basic recipe 1. The breadcrumbs will give you a lighter and more interesting texture, though an equally traditional pudding. Use suet or butter.

Variations

Golden Syrup Pudding: place 3 tablespoons (3 × 15 ml spoon) golden syrup in the basin before pouring in the sponge mixture, and then stir in 1 teaspoon (5 ml spoon) ginger with the last of the flour, which gives a wonderful aroma.

Marmalade Pudding: use 3 tablespoons (3 × 15 ml spoon) of the marmalade of your choice. Spoon into the basin before pouring in the sponge mixture.

Jam Pudding: add 3 tablespoons (3 × 15 ml spoon) jam (scarlet and black jams are particularly attractive). Spoon into the basin before pouring in the sponge mixture.

Ginger Pudding: this is excellent, and is made by adding 2 heaped tablespoons (2–3 × 15 ml spoon) ground ginger with the flour, and by adding 2 heaped tablespoons (2–3 × 15 ml spoon) warmed golden syrup at the end, instead of water. If you are about to go on a journey (or just love ginger!), add 1 oz (25 g) chopped stem ginger to the mixture at the end: they say that ginger prevents travel sickness.

Snowdon Pudding: climbers, physical or social, will want to make this pudding. Stud your pudding bowl first with 3 oz (75 g) stoned raisins; then add 3 oz (75 g) lemon marmalade and the grated rind of 1 lemon to the breadcrumb pudding mixture in Basic recipe 2. Steam as before.

Orange and Treacle Sponge Pudding: warm together 3 tablespoons (3 × 15 ml spoon) black treacle and the grated rind and juice of 2 oranges in a heavy saucepan. Fold in 2 tablespoons (2 × 15 ml spoon) breadcrumbs, and pour this mixture into a pudding basin before topping with your standard pudding mixture (Basic recipe 1).

ATHOLL BROSE

Serves 4

1 oz (25 g) medium oatmeal

2 tablespoons (2 × 15 ml spoon) clear honey

2 tablespoons (2 × 15 ml spoon) whisky

½ pint (300 ml) double cream

raspberries or blueberries, to taste

This is a wonderfully simple Scottish way to end a summer meal. Lowlanders can use some of the marvellous raspberries that grow so well in their gardens, and Highlanders can take to the hills for blueberries: either will do splendidly here.

Toast the oatmeal either by tossing and stirring it continuously over a medium heat in a non-stick pan, or by putting in a dish in a gentle oven and stirring occasionally. Let cool. Mix together the honey and the whisky. Whip the cream until it forms soft peaks but is not dry; then fold in the honey and whisky mixture. Leave this to chill. Just before serving, stir in the oatmeal (if you do it in advance, it will lose its crunch).

Put the raspberries or blueberries – or a mixture – into the bottom of tall glasses or bowls and spoon the Atholl Brose over. Alternatively, to make them go further, the berries can be folded into the mixture.

Atholl Brose

GRANDMOTHER'S BURNT CREAM

2 eggs

2 egg yolks

2 oz (50 g) plus 6 tablespoons (6 × 15 ml spoon) caster sugar

1 pint (600 ml) Jersey or thick double cream

1 dessertspoon (10 ml spoon) orange flower water

a little grated orange rind

a little grated lemon rind

Oven temperature:
Gas Mark 2/300°F/150°C

Although made famous by Trinity College in Cambridge this is a very old pudding to which no one can lay exclusive claim. I found three versions in the seventeenth and eighteenth century cookbook of Fletcher Christian's grandmother, one of which had caramel on the top and bottom – showing a clear link with the more European crème caramel. The early Burnt Creams were flavoured, too, and the most delicious variation uses orange flower water, which I use here. (The use of egg yolks only, rather than whole eggs, would give a superior result.)

Whisk the whole eggs, the egg yolks and 2 oz (50 g) of the sugar together until the sugar has dissolved, and then add the cream and the orange flower water. Whisk until smooth again and add the two grated rinds. Pour into six ramekin dishes.

Preheat the oven. Place the ramekins in a roasting tray and pour in hot water until it comes half-way up the sides of the ramekins. Bake in the centre of the oven for about an hour – the cream is cooked when a knife blade can be inserted into the cream and comes out clean. Allow to cool.

Pour 1 tablespoon (15 ml spoon) caster sugar on top of each cream. Place them under a hot, preheated grill until the sugar has melted together and you can no longer see separate grains, but don't let it burn. Remove and chill before serving.

BANANA BREAD AND BUTTER PUDDING

Serves 4–6

6–8 slices of white bread, generously buttered

2–3 teaspoons (2–3 × 5 ml spoon) ground cinnamon

1 very ripe banana, sliced

2 oz (50 g) raisins or sultanas

2 eggs

3 tablespoons (3 × 15 ml spoon) sugar

1 pint (600 ml) milk

Oven temperature:
Gas Mark 4/350°F/180°C

Bananas have been grown commercially for around 3,000 years, though they didn't arrive in this country until the sixteenth century. Perhaps one of the reasons why we don't have more recipes for them in British cookery is that they were a true luxury item until the Imperial Direct Line started shipping them from the West Indies in 1901. Few people realise, by the way, that the banana plant, 30-odd feet high, is not botanically speaking a tree but one of the world's largest herbs! Even fewer will deny that they make a wondrous addition to this all-time favourite pudding. For an interesting variation, toast the buttered fingers first.

Choose almost any white bread other than that from a sliced sandwich loaf, as this will become rather mushy. Sprinkle the buttered bread with the cinnamon. Remove the crusts, and cut the slices into fingers. In a small bowl, mix the sliced banana and the dried fruit well together. Beat the eggs together with the sugar and milk.

Using an oblong or square baking dish, arrange the fruit and the fingers of bread in layers. Pour in the custard mixture, and leave to stand for half an hour, pushing the top layer down under the liquid from time to time until all is absorbed. Preheat the oven. Bake for 50 minutes, until the custard is set and the bread is crisp and golden on top. Serve warm, not hot.

MY CLASSIC SUMMER PUDDING

Serves 4–6

half a large loaf of good white bread, two days old

a little butter (optional)

juice of 1 lemon

1 lb (450 g) raspberries, cleaned

1 lb (450 g) redcurrants, cleaned

2 oz (50 g) caster sugar (optional)

I developed this all-red recipe some years ago now, and it cannot be bettered. Simplicity is the secret here, and, as with all simple food, nothing is more important than that your basic ingredients are of the highest quality. The best results are obtained by making the pudding a day in advance.

Take the crusts off and slice the bread thinly. Line a deep pudding bowl with the slices, keeping a few for the lid. Try to make the lining as even as possible, trimming where necessary, and using a dab or two of butter if the bread won't stay in shape.

Squeeze the lemon juice over the fruit, and mix all together with the sugar, if desired. Fill the bread shell with the fruit, and top with a bread lid. Compress the pudding by resting a saucer or plate on the bread lid, with a weight of about 1 lb (450 g) on top. Leave in the refrigerator for at least 8 hours, or preferably overnight. Replace the saucer and the weight with an upside-down serving plate, and then invert: gently unmould your summer pudding. Serve swimming in single cream. If possible, decorate with fresh fruit and leaves.

My Classic Summer Pudding is an all-red one, but both blackcurrants and blackberries are popular and worthwhile additions. Both benefit from a very light cooking beforehand, which promotes extra juice. Mix them with any sugar you wish to use, and let them steep together for a little while. Then, cook them with no added liquid for a matter of minutes over a gentle heat, turn off and add them to your red fruit. Whatever your mixture, be careful with the amount of lemon and sugar you use, as this will necessarily vary every time.

My Winter Pudding
My Classic Summer Pudding

MY WINTER PUDDING

8 oz (225 g) self-raising flour

4 oz (100 g) beef suet

¼ pint (150 ml) milk

4½ oz (115 g) butter

1 lemon, weighing 4–5 oz (100–150 g)

4 oz (100 g) demerara sugar

6 oz (175 g) bramley apple(s), peeled, cored and segmented

2 dessertspoons (2 × 10 ml spoon) currants

2 dessertspoons (2 × 10 ml spoon) raisins or sultanas

I always wanted to make a Sussex Pond Pudding: a pudding of steamed suet crust, which encases sugar, butter and a well-cooked lemon. But I also wanted to invent a winter version of Summer Pudding. This is the result – basically a Pond Pudding with the addition of apple, currants and raisins. Don't be tempted to cheat on the cooking time as the lemon simply won't be done.

Mix the flour and suet together in a bowl. Make a softish dough with the milk. Roll the dough out into a large circle. Cut a quarter out of the circle and put to one side: this will make the lid of the pudding. Butter a 2½-pint (1.5-litre) pudding basin lavishly with a good ½ oz (15 g) of the butter. Drop your three-quarter circle of pastry into the bowl, and press the cut side together to make a perfect join.

Prick the lemon all over with a needle. Mix together the butter, sugar, apple and dried fruit. Put half in the bottom of the pastry-lined bowl. Place the lemon on top of the mixture, and then add the rest of the ingredients. Roll out the last of the pastry to make a lid, and place that on top of the pudding. Press the edges together so that the mixture is fully enclosed.

Cover the pudding with greaseproof paper or foil, pleated in the middle to allow for expansion, and then tie tightly with string under the rim. Loop the string ends over and tie on the opposite side to make a handle. Stand on a trivet or saucer in a deep saucepan and pour in boiling water until it reaches half-way up the bowl. Put on the lid. Keep at a steady simmer for 3½ hours, adding more boiling water if necessary.

When cooked, remove the foil, run a knife round the inside of the bowl, cover with a large plate and then invert and remove the bowl. Take the whole pudding to the table and cut and serve it there. Make sure everyone gets a piece of the lemon skin and a good share of its juice.

TEA-TIME AND MISCELLANEOUS

FRESH PEACH AND HAZELNUT SHORTCAKE

Serves 6 or more

6 oz (175 g) butter

4 oz (100 g) sugar

2 eggs

1 lb (450 g) self-raising flour

4 oz (100 g) packet of chopped, toasted hazelnuts

2 oz (50 g) brown sugar

4 large peaches

2 dessertspoons (2 × 10 ml spoon) lemon juice

1 heaped teaspoon (1–2 × 5 ml spoon) ground cinnamon

Oven temperature:
Gas Mark 4/350°F/180°C

Fruit shortcakes are very British, and very good, so much so that the French have been reduced to calling their version La Riposte. Serve this one at tea-time, as a splendid summer treat: a game of croquet would be a suitable way to build up the appetite!

Cream together the butter and the sugar really well, and then beat in the eggs and the flour. Put to one side in a cool place. If you have only fresh hazelnuts, toast them until brown right through, then rub off their skins and chop roughly. Mix the hazelnuts with the sugar. (You can process them in a food processor, but they should retain some texture, so don't process through to a powder.)

Preheat the oven. The peaches should be sliced coarsely. Peel them for finesse, but leaving them unpeeled, country-style, is perfectly acceptable.

Line a greased, 9-inch (23 cm) deep sandwich tin evenly with a little less than half the shortcake mixture. Sprinkle on the hazelnut mixture, and then arrange the sliced peaches evenly on that, leaving a border around the edge. Sprinkle with the lemon juice and cinnamon. Arrange the rest of the shortcake roughly over the top, so that it looks rather like a crumble mixture – it will spread and blend as it cooks.

Bake in the preheated oven for 35 minutes. You can serve the shortcake hot with custard as a pudding if you wish, though to my mind its splendour is never greater than at tea-time. It can then be served warm or cold, with any amount of cream.

SEVENTEENTH CENTURY BREAD AND CREAM CHEESECAKES

Makes 24 small cheesecakes

½ pint (300 ml) single cream

6 oz (175 g) fresh white breadcrumbs

1¼ lb (550 g) shortcrust pastry

4 oz (100 g) butter, softened

½ teaspoon (2.5 ml spoon) grated nutmeg

grated rind of 1 orange and ½ lemon

4 eggs, whisked together

either a little raspberry jam for each tart, or 4 oz (100 g) currants and 3–4 teaspoons (3–4 × 5 ml spoon) brandy

Oven temperature:
Gas Mark 4/350°F/180°C

For some typically eccentric but unknown reason, the traditional British cheesecake was cheeseless. It is the texture that is all-important. These light, golden-topped tarts were enjoyed by Pepys – as well as by many others before and since.

Bring the cream to the boil and pour over the breadcrumbs. Leave to soak for 2 hours.

You can make cheesecakes any size you wish, but remember that the bigger the tins, the fewer the cheesecakes and the longer the baking time. Roll out the shortcrust pastry and cut out circles big enough to line your bun tins. Line the tins with the pastry and chill them while preparing the filling.

Put the oven on to warm up. Beat the softened butter until it is creamy, and then add the nutmeg and the two rinds. Beat the butter into the breadcrumbs and cream, and mix well. Gradually and lightly beat the whisked eggs into the cream mixture.

If you are flavouring the cakes with jam, blob a little into the base of each tart. If you are using currants and brandy, mix them both lightly into the cheesecake mixture. Divide the mixture between the cases, and bake in the upper half of the preheated oven for 40–50 minutes. When they are firm and a light gold, they are done. Serve them warm.

Fresh Peach and Hazelnut Shortcake
Seventeenth Century Bread and Cream Cheesecakes

A GRAND FRUIT CAKE

1½ lb (675 g) salted butter

1½ lb (675 g) plain white flour

1 lb (450 g) caster sugar

8 eggs

2 lb (900 g) currants

12 oz (350 g) sultanas

12 oz (350 g) mixed peel, with lots of orange

8 oz (225 g) glacé cherries, pitted

8 oz (225 g) ground almonds

grated rind of 4 sweet oranges

grated rind of 2 lemons

½ oz (15 g) mixed ground cinnamon, nutmeg, cloves, according to taste

6 fl oz (175 ml) cognac

4 fl oz (100 ml) orange flower water

extra cognac, orange flower water or orange liqueur

Oven temperature:
Gas Mark 1/275°F/140°C

The grandest cake I ever made used this recipe. Five hexagonal tiers were iced in white wicker work and the spaces between each layer were filled with the same flowers the bride carried, so it looked like a stack of floating flower baskets, filled from the glorious Cornish garden in which the reception was held. Not only did it look wonderful, but most people asked for second helpings of the cake, almost unheard of at weddings these days.

Nothing is more disappointing than the actual cake inside many beautifully decorated celebrations for christenings and weddings, birthdays and anniversaries. But I guarantee only success with this recipe, adapted from the principles of a wedding cake recipe of Francatelli, one of Queen Victoria's most famous chefs. Moist and rather light in colour, the almonds and high fruit content keep it succulent for months, and the citrus and orange flower flavours prevent it being too sweet or sickly. Use only the very best ingredients, and whatever else you might change, don't cut down on the almonds!

This mixture makes about 10 lbs (4.5 kg) in weight, and you usually reckon on 8 servings per 1 lb (450 g) of cake. The proportions are simply reduced for smaller occasions.

Preheat the oven. Cream the butter well, add the flour, sugar and eggs, beating all the time. Gradually add all the other ingredients, mixing well. It is not necessary to use expensive brandy. Depending on taste, mix it with up to a third orange flower water.

Pour into your baking tins, which have been lined with several layers of buttered paper or buttered silicone baking paper. Bake for about 40 minutes per pound.

Once cool, remove the cakes from the tins and let them mature in a cool dark place for at least 2 weeks, feeding them occasionally. To do this, pierce the top and bottom with a skewer and pour on a few tablespoons of mixed cognac and orange flower water, cognac alone, or a sharp orange liqueur, such as Cointreau, Triple Sec or Mandarine Napoleon.

Cover with almond paste and/or icing, in your favourite way.

Note: if you soak fruit in alcohol before cooking such a cake, as it often recommended, you run the risk of colour leaking from the fruit into the icing.

FLAPJACKS

4 oz (100 g) butter

4 oz (100 g) soft brown sugar

3 oz (75 g) golden syrup

8 oz (225 g) medium or coarse oatmeal (porridge oats are suitable)

2 heaped teaspoons (2–3 × 5 ml spoon) ground ginger

Oven temperature:
Gas Mark 4/350°F/180°C

Flapjacks are one of the many modern descendants of the venerable gingerbread family. They've changed a bit since then: the original gingerbreads were made of an unleavened mixture of grated bread, ginger, liquorice, aniseed, pepper and honey, made into a stiff paste with old ale or claret, and covered with gold leaf.

Preheat the oven. Melt the butter with the sugar and the syrup in a large heavy saucepan (you will find it easier to measure golden syrup if you put the jar or tin in hot water first). Stir in the oats and ginger and mix thoroughly. Turn into a shallow, greased 8-inch (20 cm) square baking tin and smooth the top with a knife blade.

Bake in the middle of the preheated oven for 20–30 minutes until golden brown. Let it cool for 10 minutes or so before cutting into oblong bars. Only remove from the tin when completely cold.

PIKELETS

6 oz (175 g) plain flour

1 heaped teaspoon (1–2 ×
5 ml spoon) baking powder

1–2 dessertspoons (1–2 ×
10 ml spoon) sugar

a pinch of salt

1 egg

6–8 fl oz (175–240 ml)
milk

1 dessertspoon (10 ml
spoon) melted butter, plus
extra for cooking

*Some call these Scotch pancakes – I call them
delicious. You can call them what you like. Nothing is
better at tea-time on a cold day, or in summer when
you can top them with strawberries.*

Mix together the dry ingredients. Break in the
egg. Mix in the milk and add the melted butter.
Let stand for half an hour.

Cook on a lightly buttered griddle or heavy
pan, a dessertspoon (10 ml spoon) of mixture at a
time, turning just before the top dries to get the
best rise. Keep warm in a folded cloth, which
also softens them. Serve with butter, jam and
perhaps whipped cream.

*Flapjacks
Scones*

Pikelets

SCONES

1 rounded teaspoon (1–2 ×
5 ml spoon) baking powder

1 rounded teaspoon (1–2 ×
5 ml spoon) sugar

8 oz (225 g) plain flour,
sieved, plus extra for
flouring

¼ pint (150 ml) milk

a pinch of salt

Oven temperature:
Gas Mark 7/425°F/220°C

Scones are one of the cornerstones of the British baking tradition, and grandchildren all across the land remember their grandmother and great-aunts for their warm tea-time scones, fresh from the oven. They are essentially very simple to make, but, as with most simple things, it's the small touches that distinguish the great from the less great; the supergranny from the ordinary granny. Here are a few tips of my own.

The main secret of good, light scones is to have all the ingredients and equipment nice and warm before you start. (Pop them briefly in the oven.) Also, the exact proportion of liquid to flour is impossible to give, as flour is notorious for never absorbing the same amount of liquid – that even goes for branded flours.

Preheat the oven. Warm all the ingredients slightly; the flour particularly lightly. Mix all the dry ingredients together and add the milk. Work in quickly to make a light, soft dough. Add more milk or flour if the mixture is too dry or too sloppy.

Tip the mixture on to a lightly floured surface and knock the edges gently to make an oblong shape. Do not pat the top or you will knock out the air. Cut the scone mixture into squares using the sharpest knife you can lay your hands on. (Do not use a blunt knife or cake cutters, as these will press and flatten the mixture.)

Sprinkle the scones generously with flour and quickly arrange them on a preheated baking tray. Use a palette knife or slice to avoid handling the scones themselves. Bake undisturbed in the preheated oven for 15–20 minutes, according to how big you made them.

When the scones are baked, put them on a rack and cover with a clean cloth if you like a soft scone; leave uncovered, though, for the hint of a crust. Pull open rather than cut with a knife.

Scone Variations

'Keeping' Scones: the scone recipe above makes wonderfully light and airy scones, as they are made without fat. To make a more 'keeping' scone, rub in 2–3 oz (50–75 g) butter to the dry ingredients before you add the milk. If you like a 'short' taste, use lard rather than butter.

Spice Scones: mix in 1 teaspoon (5 ml spoon) cinnamon and ½ teaspoon (2.5 ml spoon) each of ground ginger and nutmeg to your basic mixture.

Orange and Vanilla Scones: this hauntingly-flavoured scone has the grated rind of 1 large orange mixed into the basic mixture, together with ½–1 teaspoon (1–2 × 2.5 ml spoon) vanilla essence.

Coconut Scones: these are delicious. Mix in 6 tablespoons (6 × 5 ml spoon), or even more, toasted desiccated coconut.

Savoury Cheese Scones: mix in 3–4 oz (75–100 g) finely grated, farmhouse Cheddar cheese, either all into the mixture, or reserving some to sprinkle on top for a cheese crust.

A SIMPLE TEA CAKE

2½–3 oz (65–70 g) butter, plus extra for greasing

3 oz (75 g) caster sugar, plus an extra heaped teaspoon (1–2 × 5 ml spoon)

1 egg

5 oz (150 g) plain flour

4 fl oz (110 ml) milk

a few drops of vanilla essence

1 heaped teaspoon (1–2 × 5 ml spoon) baking powder

1 heaped teaspoon (1–2 × 5 ml spoon) cinnamon

1 heaped teaspoon (1–2 × 5ml spoon) cocoa powder

Oven temperature:
Gas Mark 5/375°F/190°C

Here is a simple cutting cake with an unusual topping. It is best served fresh, and is the ideal thing for unexpected tea-time guests.

Preheat the oven. Beat together 1 oz (25 g) of the butter and the 3 oz (75 g) caster sugar. When they are fully creamed, beat in the egg, and then the flour, milk and vanilla essence by turns. Beat in the baking powder with the last of the flour. Pour the mixture into a buttered, shallow 8-inch (20 cm) sandwich tin and smooth, banking slightly to the outside. Bake in the preheated oven for about 30 minutes, testing to see if it is done with a fork or skewer.

When the tea cake is cooked, take it out of the oven, invert it on to your hand or a plate and then on to a cake rack, so that it is the right way up. Mix together the extra spoon of sugar, the cinnamon and the cocoa. Butter the top while it is still warm with the remaining 1½–2 oz (40–50 g) butter, and then sieve on the remaining mixed dry ingredients. Cut into 8–10 slices and serve, still warm if possible.

Boiled Fruit Cake
A Simple Tea-cake

BOILED FRUIT CAKE

Makes a 7–8-inch (18–20 cm) cake

12 oz (350 g) mixed dried fruit

4 oz (100 g) butter

4 oz (100 g) demerara sugar

¼ pint (150 ml) water

8 oz (225 g) self-raising flour, sifted

1 teaspoon (5 ml spoon) mixed spice

2 eggs, beaten lightly

Oven temperatures:
Gas Mark 3/325°F/170°C
Gas Mark 2/300°F/150°C

Tea-time isn't tea-time without a fruit cake. This one is famous for being reliable all around what used to be the British Empire.

Put the fruit, butter, sugar and water in a large, sturdy saucepan. Bring just up to the boil, stirring well. Simmer gently for 20 minutes or so, stirring from time to time to make sure that the mixture doesn't stick.

After the 20 minutes is up, remove from the heat and let the mixture cool for half an hour. Preheat the oven to the higher setting. Then add the sifted flour, the spice and the lightly beaten eggs. Mix them all together well and pour into a lined 7–8-inch (18–20 cm) cake tin. Bake in the middle of the preheated oven for half an hour, then reduce the heat to the lower setting and continue baking for another 1½ hours. Cool the cake in the tin for 10–15 minutes before turning out on to a rack to cool.

SKIRLIE

Serves 2–4

2 oz (50 g) beef dripping or suet

4 oz (100 g) onion, chopped finely

4 oz (100 g) medium or coarse oatmeal

salt and pepper, to taste

For a really traditional taste of old Scotland, try this Aberdeenshire oatmeal recipe. It's a marvellous example of that particularly Scottish combination of the rich and savoury with the economical and nourishing. Skirlie is traditionally somewhat dry, but you may add a little butter or oil if you like.

Heat the beef dripping or suet very well in a thick pan. Add the onion and brown thoroughly. When browned, add the oatmeal, turn the heat down and continue to cook gently for a minute or so while the oatmeal crisps up. Season. Serve with mince and/or potatoes to be traditional; sprinkle on to soup or mix through a green salad to be contemporary.

WELSH RABBIT

4 oz (100 g) Lancashire or strong Cheddar cheese, grated

3 tablespoons (3 × 15 ml spoon) ale

a knob of butter

1 teaspoon (5 ml spoon) English mustard

2 slices of brown bread

salt and pepper

Rabbit, the Welsh say, not rarebit (in fact what they say is caws pobi), and as they've been eating it since the fourteenth century, they should know. The Victorians, upstairs and down, loved toasted cheese, and as well as toasting it on bread and other dishes they went to enormous lengths to melt it satisfactorily so that they could dip bread, fondue-like, into it. No Briton, of course, could ever forget Ben Gunn's poignant lament, after three years marooned on Treasure Island: 'Well, many's the long night I've dreamed of cheese – toasted, mostly . . .'

Melt the cheese with the ale in a heavy saucepan over a very low heat. Add the knob of butter, mustard, salt and pepper.

Toast the slices of bread, pour the cheese mixture over them and put under a fierce grill for a few seconds while the cheese bubbles and browns. Serve immediately.

The regionally minded can ring the changes by making Scotch rabbit, with Dunlop cheese and 1 oz (25 g) butter. Irish rabbit is made with Guinness and 1 oz (25 g) chopped pickled gherkin, and Yorkshire rabbit (or Buck rabbit) is made by using Wensleydale cheese and topping with a poached egg.

YORKSHIRE PUDDING

Serves 6–8

4 oz (100 g) plain flour

¼ teaspoon (1.25 ml spoon) salt

2 eggs

¼ pint (150 ml) milk

¼ pint (150 ml) water

Oven temperature:
Gas Mark 8/450°F/230°C

Although the principles of how to cook Yorkshire pudding are well known, there still exists a lot of confusion about when to cook it. In the old days, of course, it was always cooked under the joint, and collected the dripping rendered by the joint as it cooked. (This method dates from the eighteenth century, when the recipe first became popular.) However, contemporary pudding eaters are unlikely to have the appetites of their hard-working forbears, nor is there the same pressing need to blunt the appetite before the meat arrives (Yorkshire pudding was originally served before the meat, so that less meat would feed more). A less fatty, lighter, puffier pudding is now preferred, and the perfect time for this to cook is during the 20 minutes or half-hour when the joint is (or should be!) standing after being roasted. Do remember to use dripping to make the pudding: the flavour will benefit from it. And, bring it straight from the oven to the table – everyone should show off once in a while.

Make a well in the centre of the flour. Scatter the salt around the edge. Mix together the milk and water. Put the eggs and a little of the milky water in the centre of the flour well. Mix, and continue mixing as you gradually add the rest of the milky water.

Preheat the oven. Spoon 1 teaspoon (5 ml spoon) of the fat from the meat, or use good dripping, and pour into (ideally) two small heavy dishes, or one larger one, placed on a baking tray. Heat them to smoking in the oven. Pour in the pudding mixture and cook for 20 minutes, or for 30 minutes if you're using a single dish. No peeping for the first 15 minutes!

GRAVY

Good gravy is a natural expression of the meat you have just cooked, combined with the fats, vegetables and herbs you have used in cooking. It can be extended by the liquid of your choice – water, stock or wine.

The two basic techniques you need to make good gravy are those of deglazing and reducing. When your joint is cooked, remove it from its cooking tray and let it stand for at least 20 minutes in a warmish place – the meat will be much better for this rest. Spoon off all the fat that you don't want, and deglaze the tray by pouring in a small amount of liquid and scraping up the roasting juices as you do so. Pour this basic gravy into a saucepan, together with more water, stock or wine (about ¼–½ pint/150–300 ml). Reduce it by cooking over a high heat, stirring to help evaporation. This will concentrate the natural flavour of your gravy. Keep reducing until you have the flavour and volume you want. And that's it.

That said, there are a couple of further tips that will help you on the road to good gravy. If you don't have wine or a good stock for your gravy, you'll have to use water – so to give the gravy enough flavour you'll need a lot of browning left in the roasting tray. Achieve this by putting something underneath the joint while roasting, such as sliced onion or sliced root vegetables, or perhaps a bunch of mint for lamb. If you have a liquidiser, you can even use these vegetables later to thicken the gravy: it will then have much more flavour than if it was thickened by cornflour.

Finally, gravy should complement and enhance the natural flavour of your meat, not drown it. A few spoonsful of well–reduced, unthickened, perhaps wine-accented pan juices will do this perfectly.

WHITE SAUCE

1 pint (600 ml) milk

1 bay leaf

5 peppercorns, crushed lightly

2 allspice berries, crushed lightly

1 oz (25 g) onion, sliced

1 oz (25 g) butter

1 oz (25 g) plain flour

½ teaspoon (2.5 ml spoon) salt

½ teaspoon (2.5 ml spoon) pepper

White sauce is one of the few sauces known well and used widely in every major European culinary tradition. The French call it béchamel, *the Italians* balsamella. *It is a simple sauce to master, and one of the most useful, since there are so many successful variations. Here is a basic recipe, followed by some of the simplest and most fundamental variations. The one secret is to be sure to flavour the milk first – you'll never sneer again.*

Bring the milk to the boil with the bay leaf, peppercorns, allspice berries and onion. When it has boiled, turn it off and leave it to steep for 15 minutes.

Meanwhile, melt the butter over a low heat in a heavy saucepan. Add the flour, and stir over a low heat until you have an absolutely smooth mixture that foams gently: this will take 1–1½ minutes. Under no circumstances let the flour brown.

Strain the milk, and add it bit by bit to the sauce, stirring until each addition is fully absorbed before adding the next. When all the milk is absorbed, add the salt and pepper and then simmer for 3 minutes, stirring almost continually. It is best to allow the sauce to sit over a very low heat for 15 minutes to develop its flavour fully. You now have a basic white sauce of a coating consistency, suitable, for example, for serving with light fish or meat dishes. For a thicker sauce – to use in a baked pasta dish, for instance – continue to simmer, stirring from time to time, until it has reduced to the consistency you require.

White Sauce Variations

Quick White Sauce: use 2 rounded tablespoons
(2–3 × 15 ml spoon) cornflour to thicken the
milk: mix the cornflour with a little milk before
adding to the rest of the warmed milk, and then
return to the heat to cook through.

Slimmers' White Sauce: use the basic recipe above,
but use skimmed milk rather than whole milk.

Cream Sauce: use the basic recipe above but make
it only with ½ pint (300 ml) milk. Then,
increase the sauce by adding single or double
cream until you have the consistency you need.

Wine Sauce: use the basic recipe above, and then
add ¼ pint (150 ml) or more white wine after the
sauce is finished, and then reduce over a medium
heat to your preferred consistency.

Parsley Sauce: add at least 1 oz (25 g) finely
chopped parsley to the recipe, after it has
simmered for the 3 minutes.

Cheese Sauce: add at least 4 oz (100 g) very finely
grated farmhouse Cheddar cheese, and 1 teaspoon (5 ml spoon) mustard, to the finished
basic recipe. You might also add a little Tabasco,
cayenne pepper or nutmeg to a cheese sauce, if
you wish.

Whether you're a keen gardener or merely a keen shopper, it always seems a shame to let the abundance of summer fruits that we enjoy in this country pass by without saving some for winter. The freezer is one answer, though it can become monotonous, and soft fruits in particular are often not the same after a sub-zero journey. Jam is another good solution – so long as you like jam day after day.

Now imagine the delights of sipping a glass of raspberry vodka or blueberry gin on a rainy November evening or a sleety January one, with the spirit-charged fruits themselves to sprinkle on hot gammon or cold ice cream. *That's* the way to remember last summer. Slimmers and teetotallers can console themselves with fruit vinegars, either as Victorian-style drinks or in salads and contemporary sauces.

Alcohols and Liqueurs

There are no absolute rules about making your own fruit-flavoured alcohols and liqueurs, or vinegars for that matter. Starting with alcohols and liqueurs, the first thing that has to be decided is whether you are going to make a dry brandy-style drink, or a sweeter liqueur-style drink.

The best fruits to use are berry fruits, such as raspberries, strawberries, blackberries, black-currants, and so on, but you may also like to experiment with other soft fruit, such as damsons, plums, apricots, peaches and cherries.

THE BASIC PROPORTIONS

1 lb (450 g) fruit

1 pint (600 ml) alcohol (brandy, gin, vodka or whisky)

4 oz (100 g) sugar for a dry spirit, up to 12 oz (350 g) sugar for a liqueur-style drink

Never crush your fruit, but if you are using a tough-skinned fruit, like damsons or sloes, either prick them or cut into slices. For strawberries, halve. For peaches, leave the skins on, but halve and remove the stones.

Put the fruit in a clean jar with a firm top,

The Twelvemonth Summer

layering with the sugar. Then pour on the brandy, gin, vodka or whisky. Keep in a cool dark place and give it a few turns every day for a couple of weeks until the sugar has dissolved. Keep for 2–3 months to get the best results – it will be worth the willpower, I promise.

Serve the alcohol chilled as an aperitif; serve the sweeter liqueur after a meal. Both make sensational additions to a glass of champagne, especially the liqueurs. And, of course, fruit such as peaches, raspberries, blackberries and blackcurrants will, after this treatment, lift even the most uninspiring pudding into the realms of the sublime. Use them more cautiously with meats and savoury courses, wherever you feel the alcoholic fruit will highlight rather than dominate – for example, with gammon or hams, duck or geese, rich game or a grand piece of lamb. Your guests will be in ecstasy – mine were.

You can make far smaller quantities than those above by dividing the recipe, but maintaining the proportions: 8 oz (225 g) fruit to ½ pint (300 ml) liquor, for example. But don't worry: you can add more or less of anything without having a disaster.

Fruit Vinegars

Delicious fruit vinegars can be made by steeping 1 lb (450 g) of the fruit of your choice in 1 pint (600 ml) vinegar (white wine or cider). Leave in a warm place for 7 days or so. If you wish for a strong fruit-flavoured vinegar, strain off the wine or vinegar and repeat the process with the same amount of fresh fruit again. Raspberry vinegar is one of the best and most successful of these – it is superb with beans or raw spinach – but once again it's up to you to experiment.

As well as fruits, you could try using wild flowers – elderflower will give you a lovely muscatel flavour – or herbs. The more you use, the stronger the flavour will be. The Victorians used to sweeten their fruit vinegars with sugar, and then make them into refreshing summer drinks with iced soda water. Try it – and combine the traditional and the exotic!

INDEX TO RECIPES

Design and layout: Ken Vail Graphic Design
Photography: John Lee, Steven Lee and Melvin Grey
Home economists: Ann Page-Wood, Jacqui Hine and Jane Suthering
Illustrations: Richard Jacobs
Typesetting: Westholme Graphics Limited, Gamlingay, Beds
Printed and bound by Balding & Mansell Ltd, Wisbech, Cambs